Handbook for Teeline Teachers

Edited by

HARRY
BUTLER

D1471633

 Heinemann Educational Books

Other Teeline titles

Teeline: Revised Edition by I. C. Hill and Meriel Bowers
Teeline Shorthand Made Simple by Harry Butler
Teeline Word List by I. C. Hill
First Teeline Workbook: Revised Edition by I. C. Hill and Meriel Bowers
Second Teeline Workbook: Revised Edition by I. C. Hill and Meriel Bowers
Teeline Shorthand Dictation Passages edited by Dorothy Bowyer
Teeline Dictation and Drill Book by I. C. Hill and G. S. Hill

Heinemann Educational Books Ltd
22 Bedford Square, London WC1B 3HH

LONDON   EDINBURGH   MELBOURNE   AUCKLAND
HONG KONG   SINGAPORE   KUALA LUMPUR   NEW DELHI
IBADAN   NAIROBI   JOHANNESBURG
PORTSMOUTH (NH)   KINGSTON

© Harry Butler 1983
First published 1983
Reprinted 1986

British Library Cataloguing in Publication Data

Handbook for Teeline teachers.
1. Shorthand – Teeline
I Butler, Harry, 19—
653'.478   Z56.2.T4
ISBN 0-435-45310-6

Filmset in 'Monophoto' Ehrhardt
by Eta Services (Typesetters) Ltd., Beccles, Suffolk
Printed in Great Britain by Biddles Ltd., Guildford

Contents

Contributors

DIANA AIREY learned Teeline on a TOPS course, thinking she might 'do' something in an office while the children were at school. She began to teach at two evening classes and the hours increased with the demand for Teeline. For many years, she was a full-time lecturer teaching Teeline to trainee journalists at the London College of Printing.

PAUL BERRY was formerly senior lecturer and Deputy Head of the Secretarial Studies Department at Kingsway-Princeton College, London, where he taught Teeline for twelve years with outstanding success.

PEGGY BLACKHURST has taught in both primary and secondary schools. As Head of Business Studies in schools in Surrey and Sussex, she has introduced and taught Teeline since 1969.

NANCY BLAIR is senior lecturer in the Commerce Department at Anniesland College, Glasgow, and has specialized in teaching medical secretaries.

MERIEL BOWERS, lecturer and course tutor for RSA and FTC Teachers' Diplomas at Huddersfield Technical College, has been teaching Teeline at all levels since 1970. She is co-author of *Teeline Revised Edition*.

DOROTHY BOWYER, formerly lecturer and course tutor at Sutton Coldfield College of Further Education, taught secretarial subjects for many years and Teeline from 1971. She is a chief examiner in shorthand for the London Chamber of Commerce and Industry (LCCI).

FRANCES J. BURTON is senior lecturer in the Department of Business and Management Studies at Oxford College of Further Education. She is co-author of the German adaptation of Teeline.

HARRY BUTLER is the author of many books on shorthand and journalism and is Teeline lecturer at the Graduate Centre for Journalism, City University, London. For 25 years he was shorthand consultant to the National Council for the Training of Journalists (NCTJ).

JEAN CLARKSON is Group Shorthand Tutor for United Newspapers Training Department in North West Lancashire. She is chairman of the Shorthand Examinations Board of the NCTJ.

ANN DIX joined the BBC Office Training Department as an instructor in 1967 and has taught Teeline since 1970. From 1980–84 she was senior instructor responsible for day-to-day administration and the running of courses, as well as teaching Teeline to new instructors joining the department. She now teaches Teeline at the Centre for Journalism Studies, City University, London.

DOROTHY FORD, Cert. Ed., F.S.C.T., F.F.T.Com., was until recently senior lecturer at Richmond College of Further Education, Sheffield. She has had forty years' experience teaching shorthand in further education establishments and is a member of the Executive Council of the Society of Teachers in Business Education.

RUTH FRYER, Cert. Ed., F.S.C.T., has been teaching shorthand for many years in schools, to journalists and for the last ten years at Orpington College of Further Education, Kent. There she teaches Teeline on the one-year courses for the LCCI Private Secretary's Certificate and the Secretarial Studies Certificate.

ANN HARVEY is senior lecturer at Oxford College of Further Education and has written the French adaptation of Teeline. She is also co-author of *Devenez Secretaire Bilingue* (Cassell), a textbook for bilingual secretaries.

JUNE HASKELL is an instructor at Spelthorne Adult Education Institute, The Oast House, Staines, Middlesex, where she has specialized in teaching courses under the Training Opportunities Scheme (TOPS).

GEORGE HILL, B.A., is a former Teeline instructor at the Centre for Journalism Studies, University of Wales, Cardiff, and chief examiner for Teeline Education Ltd. He is the son of the inventor of Teeline.

I. C. HILL, D.C.P., F.S.C.T., F.F.T.Com., author of many Teeline books, has had long and varied teaching experience in both general and commercial subjects. She is the holder of the Alfred Pitman Prize for 1949, awarded to the candidate placed first in the UK in the Pitman's Shorthand Teacher's Diploma for that year.

PAULINE HOSKING, Dip. RSA, F.S.C.T., has taught shorthand since 1950 in secondary schools and in colleges of further education in various parts of the country and was Head of the Department of Business Studies at Seven Kings High School, Ilford, Essex. While there, she converted to Teeline. A member of the Executive Council of the Society of Teachers in Business Education, she was Chairwoman of the London District in 1982–3.

JOAN McCLUNG, B.Ed., F.S.C.T., co-author of the Spanish adaptation of Teeline, is senior lecturer at the College of Business

Studies, Belfast. She changed to Teeline in 1971 and has been teaching it successfully since then.

SARAH McGHEE, a lecturer for many years in the Department of Office Organization, University of Strathclyde, Glasgow, used to teach students on the Postgraduate Diploma in Secretarial Studies. The changeover to Teeline took place in 1975. The B.A. degree course converted to Teeline in October 1983.

MURIEL O'DONNELL learned Teeline on a TOPS course at Spelthorne Adult Education Institute at Staines, Middlesex, and now teaches it on TOPS courses there.

ROBERT ORR, B.A., Dip. Ed., D.B.A., co-author of the Spanish adaptation of Teeline, is senior lecturer in Modern Languages in the Department of Secretarial Studies at the College of Business Studies, Belfast.

CELIA OSBORNE has taught Teeline at all levels from school-leavers with a few CSEs to postgraduates on the intensive secretarial course at the City of London Polytechnic. She has also taught journalists and has trained three other contributors to this book.

ULRIKE PARKINSON, a lecturer at Oxford College of Further Education, is author of the tapes used in connection with German Teeline. She was also the teacher of Tracy McGregor who won the 1983 £1000 Teeline Shorthand Competition with a speed of 170 w.p.m.

Teeline Addresses

Teeline speed examinations

Teeline Education Ltd offer a 'round-the-year' speed examinations service to any recognized educational institution. Speeds range from 50–160 w.p.m. (in tens).

- *Stage 1*   50, 60 and 70 w.p.m.
- *Stage 2*   80, 90 and 100 w.p.m.
- *Stage 3*   110 and 120 w.p.m.
- *Stage 4*   130 and 140 w.p.m.
- *Stage 5*   150 and 160 w.p.m.

Minimum number of entries per examination: four
Specimen examination passages: one booklet available for each stage except Stage 5.
For full details of examinations, application forms or specimen booklets, please contact: The Examinations Officer, Teeline Education Ltd, First Floor, 5 Wellfield Road, Cardiff CF2 3NZ (tel. 0222 465398).

The Teeline Association

This is an organization for people interested in Teeline—teachers, students and Teeline writers. Members receive a quarterly newsletter. Membership forms available from: The Membership Secretary, The Teeline Association, c/o The Oast House, Kingston Road, Staines, Middlesex TW18 4LP.

The Teeline Magazine

Teeline: the shorthand and business studies magazine is published on the first Friday of every month by Jazz Journal Ltd, 35 Great Russell Street, London WC1B 3PP (tel. 01-580 7244). The magazine can be ordered through any newsagent or on subscription from the publishers.

Foreword

HARRY BUTLER

This book presents a symposium of views on teaching Teeline by tutors who, through their expertise and scholarship, have for many years been in the vanguard of successful instructors.

Its aim is twofold. First, to present to experienced teachers a freshening of ideas and the possibility of a new approach to the subject. Second, to offer guidance to those who are thinking of becoming instructors or are preparing for the Royal Society of Arts Teachers' Diploma in Shorthand (Teeline) or the Faculty of Teachers in Commerce Diploma in Teeline.

There is an abundance of knowledge and know-how, the summation of wide experience, in all the contributions on the following pages. Even those who have been giving Teeline tuition since the earliest days of the system will find themselves mentally invigorated as they read.

The first part of this handbook presents the views and advice of people who are experts in their own fields. The majority of them have quite deliberately changed to Teeline from other systems, and the satisfaction they have gained by doing so is evident from their writings.

Occasionally, the chapters show variations in the approach to teaching Teeline. Some lecturers prefer to present the entire alphabet at the beginning; others give only selected letters, or introduce the consonants and leave the vowels until later. There are teachers who like to introduce certain principles, such as the use of TR for THR, earlier than they are given in the textbooks. There is nothing wrong in this, and it demonstrates that there is as much freedom in the teaching of Teeline as there is in the writing of it.

The plurality of outlines sometimes found in the system is often looked upon with suspicion by pre-Teeline teachers who regard any departure from a dictionary form as heresy; yet this ability to write a word more than one way and still be 'correct' is perfectly logical, as will be shown presently.

Anybody who has ever tried to devise a shorthand alphabet knows that the job is anything but easy, and the would-be inventor ends up with a greater admiration than before for those who have succeeded in doing so. Since 1588 there have been nearly 500 shorthand methods of various sorts published in Britain and probably as many again in the United States and other parts of the English-speaking world. Not one of them has been like Teeline, which approaches the task of fast writing from a new angle.

Teeline shorthand breaks fresh ground in that it concentrates on the streamlining of longhand letters rather than allocating isolated strokes which are unlike their handwritten counterparts.

By constructing his alphabet from our normal lettering, James Hill immediately cut down the amount of time usually taken to learn basic shorthand symbols. Teachers of Teeline will be familiar with the alacrity shown by students in writing them and will know that they are learned with barely a second glance.

This is because, as several contributors point out, pupils proceed from the known to the unknown from the first lesson. There are several ways of writing many letters in our longhand and one does not have to look far to find a few of them. I make use of two ways for writing an 's' and two ways for writing an 'r'. They are interchangeable and I never know which one is coming off the tip of my pen until it has been written. Other people have similar habits, yet these variants of 's' or 'r' or 'b' or 'k' which we all use cannot be mistaken for any other letter and they are easily recognized by those who read our writing.

If we do this in our longhand, then it is logical that we should carry the habit into our shorthand; and just as there is no mistaking the letters in ordinary writing, so there is no mistaking the variants in Teeline.

The principle of streamlining goes through the entire system. When we write longhand hurriedly, the letters blend into one another. If we speedily jot down the word *coming*, for example, we probably write *com* clearly, but in our haste the *-ing* is reduced to a short line followed by a 'g', but the word can only be read as *coming*. This streamlining or blending is put to good use in Teeline and it is one of the first things a teacher brings to the notice of a class. It is also something that students of all ages are quick to grasp.

Although this is a book for teachers, it will be as well to bear in mind the reaction of pupils to Teeline. During the time I have been teaching it, whether to graduates, adults, teachers of other systems or to teenagers, I have always sought their views on the system. They have said they have found it: 1. logical and therefore easy to learn; 2. simpler than other systems, but just as fast; 3. 'straightforward' (i.e. no complexities); 4. there is nothing to 'unlearn'.

The latter point is one that causes dissension among a minority of Teeline teachers, usually those who have converted from other systems. It is the reason why some of them prefer to introduce a few principles earlier than they are given in the textbooks. The use of the TR blend for THR (as in *bother, mother, weather*) mentioned earlier, is a case in point. They consider it should be introduced early so that students should not have to write *bother, mother, weather* and similar words with a TH and a stroke R. Their argument is that if students start using the TH and the separate R, then they have to 'unlearn' this when they come to the extended use of the TR blend. Another example is the omission of L in most words ending in '-ly' (*cleary* for *clearly*, *eventy* for *eventually*, *variousy* for *variously*, etc.).

Surely, on reflection, they must see that there is no 'unlearning'. When a child first starts to write, it learns that A–N–D spells *and*; later it finds that the ampersand can be used for the word, thus streamlining it, and thereafter it uses both. There has been no 'unlearning' – merely an adaptation. It is the same with other forms of letters in handwriting, such as the 's' and the 'r' referred to above. The child is simply made aware of the differences and uses them or not, by choice.

It is the same with Teeline outlines. Students learn the simple way first and write *bother* and *mother* and *weather* with the TH and the R. Later comes the extension of the TR blend to include THR, and it is up to them to use it or not. They do not *have* to use it and they should not be made to do so. My own experience, for what it is worth, is that some take to it and others do not, and the glorious freedom of Teeline allows them a choice they would not find elsewhere.

Teachers can present the Teeline principles in any order they like – they are free to do so – but students also have a freedom of choice and if they decide not to make use of some of the principles, that is up to them.

The wise teacher will be firm in giving guidance, but the final decision must rest with the student, and the teacher well versed in Teeline will be aware that even the basics of the system are sufficient for anyone to achieve a speed usable in the office.

In the end it is the student who will provide results. A teacher will work hard instructing and guiding, but if a student does not make sufficient effort, in most cases a satisfactory speed will not be reached. The words 'in most cases' are the important ones here, because there are occasions when even hard-working students will be limited by a lack of vocabulary. I have in mind a young graduate who had never heard of a tombola, and when it was explained she said incredulously 'Oh – bingo!' People for whom English is a second language will also have vocabulary difficulties, and this is touched upon by Pauline Hosking in Chapter 4. Several years ago I had a young Chinese journalist as a student. His application to Teeline was quite surprising and he was frequently ahead of his English colleagues. But try as he might, he could not get beyond 60 w.p.m. His perfect, precise English was one thing, but commonplace expressions were quite something else. When he heard *all at sea*, *in at the deep end*, or *a different cup of tea* his pen stopped. He knew all the individual words, but the colloquialisms were something new and therefore beyond him until they were explained. His speed might only have been 60 w.p.m., but he went away with a better grasp of everyday English.

Throughout the contributions in Part One of this book there is one common theme and that is the importance of transcription practice. Of all the subsidiary skills connected with shorthand this is the most neglected, yet it is by the transcript that shorthand ability must be judged. Anyone can fill pages of a notebook with scribble and call it shorthand, but those hieroglyphics are only useful if and when they can be transcribed properly and perfectly.

'Writing back' is a chore just as much as learning irregular verbs, and it is just as necessary. There is no short cut. Reading back in class is no substitute, for although this assists the speedy recognition of outlines, it does not provide a check on spelling or punctuation.

This is something teachers often talk about, but as an examiner I often suspect that the need for regular transcription practice is only given lip-service, and the advice is proffered rather than the act performed. Fortunately Teeline is a system in which transcription on a wide vocabulary can be commenced in the earliest lessons, and if this is followed through in one of the ways suggested by contributors, examiners may in future be able to award a pass to even more candidates.

The failure rate in shorthand speed tests has always been high, but with an examinations board with which I am connected (that of the National Council for the Training of Journalists), the failure rate in Teeline is *lower* than with other systems. This has been the case ever since Teeline was first published, but, even so, failures still amount to nearly two-thirds the number of candidates. This is a disconcertingly large proportion, though it is not as high as in other systems examined by the board. A scrutiny of papers shows that some candidates entered (or were entered) before they were ready for the test, and doubtless there were those who relied more on inspiration than on perspiration (a common failing, it seems, among trainee journalists and graduates); but there were many who, having written a perfectly good note, were unable to read it.

This indicates only one thing: a lack of transcription practice, and on this point the comments of Meriel Bowers (Chapter 2), Paul Berry (Chapter 6), Sarah McGhee (Chapter 7) and in particular George Hill (Chapter 17) are worth reading more than once.

The intention of most people who take up shorthand voluntarily is to use it as a means of earning a living. Admirable though this may be, the resolution rapidly diminishes as soon as a little difficulty is encountered, and teachers find attendance dwindling. With Teeline this does not happen so much. Its simplicity and logicality have a universal appeal, with the result that progress is quicker and drop-outs are fewer. This is welcomed by teachers who have changed to Teeline and can therefore make comparisons with their previous classes. For them, the achievements of Teeline are especially impressive. Those who are teaching in evening institutes (or are intending to do so) will find Dorothy Bowyer's contribution (Chapter 14) of value. Her final words:

'Teeline generates so much interest among students . . .' apply not only to evening classes. Whenever the system is taught, teachers notice that a higher proportion of pupils become enthusiastic about Teeline than can be found with other systems.

I first taught Teeline before the early textbook was published, when the system comprised six lessons. They are in front of me now, headed 'Correspondence Course in Basic Teeline'. The entire system is contained in nineteen foolscap pages with outlines inserted by hand, and a total of eighteen exercises, most of them run off on a spirit duplicator.

Looking at these now-precious sheets (for few of them could have survived the years) one is struck by how little the system has changed, which says much for the care and ingenuity with which James Hill constructed it. What has happened is that in the interim the presentation of Teeline has become more refined; more examples are given; exercises are longer and more comprehensive. All this makes learning easier. In this early course, the blending of R with T and D, the TRN and DRN blends, the blending of R with L, M and W, and the blending of F with other consonants were presented in one and a half pages of foolscap. Today, they are spread over several chapters to allow teachers greater flexibility in instruction and students more opportunity for assimilation.

In his introduction to the course James Hill wrote: 'In a correspondence course these six lessons might reasonably be spread over about twelve weeks, assuming about four hours' work per unit' – a total of 48 hours, and as a matter of fact, my first Teeline class not only got through the lessons in 36 hours, but were capable of passing internal examinations at 70 to 90 w.p.m. for five minutes.

The class was organized by the National Council for the Training of Journalists – probably the first national body to realize the potentialities of Teeline – and I was asked to conduct it. Among the students was Florence Carter, a former head of the BBC Office Training Department, who achieved 90 w.p.m. As a result, the BBC discarded the system previously taught and went over to Teeline. In Chapter 11, Ann Dix, former senior instructor, writes of the consistent success the BBC has had with Teeline.

In addition, she gives detailed timetables for the presentation of Teeline on various courses, which will be of considerable use and guidance to those who find themselves facing the prospect of teaching a crash course for the first time. The experience Ann Dix has had in conducting such courses, and of tutoring on company block-release schemes, is here shared with readers, to whom it will be of immeasurable benefit.

Every facet of teaching Teeline has been covered, as a perusal of the chapter headings will show. There are also sections on keeping class records; the examiner's point of view; converting to Teeline; team teaching; and the position of Teeline in the technological age. The chapter on this latter subject, by Dorothy Ford, provides an unanswerable argument for the adoption of Teeline. It is particularly commended and makes a fitting conclusion to Part One of the book.

Part Two deals with preparation for teaching qualifications in Teeline such as the Royal Society of Arts Teachers' Diploma in Shorthand (Teeline), and the Faculty of Teachers in Commerce Teacher's Diploma in Teeline. Meriel Bowers who has written the part dealing with the RSA Diploma has much experience in Teeline teacher training and as an examiner for independent public examining bodies. Part Two will be of value not only to the newcomer to teaching, but to those instructors who accept the challenge of testing their own ability and improving their standards by taking these examinations.

This is not a book to read and put down. It is a book to re-read from time to time with profit and pleasure.

One final suggestion: do not lend this copy to anyone, for you may never get it back!

PART ONE

Chapter 1 How Teeline Began

I. C. HILL

Teeline is the result of work study principles being applied to handwriting. This means removing from ordinary longhand all unnecessary letters from words, all unnecessary parts of ordinary written or printed characters, and all unnecessary movements in joining letters together.

These three steps reduce what is normally written by more than half. Once these steps have been mastered, a wide vocabulary is opened up and exercise material can be interesting and meaningful. The student has a sense of immediate achievement, which stimulates the desire to learn, and handwriting speed can be doubled or trebled.

Teeline also makes use of standard contractions and abbreviations, of the principles of blending letters together and of grouping words where they form recognized speech patterns. Contracting devices are also used for word beginnings and word endings. The use of initials, numbers and fractions, and metric measurement signs all help to reduce further the amount that needs to be written.

Teeline is based on spelling but it is phonetic in so far as the alphabet is phonetic. For instance, C and K, G and J often have the same sound in words, so if it is easier to substitute C for K or G for J, then this can be done. Where PH and GH have the sound of F, then F is used because this is quicker and easier than writing two letters. Similarly, one letter may be used to represent a whole syllable. For example, S is used for the sound SHL and N for the sound of -TION, regardless of spelling.

Although ordinary handwriting style can be retained, Teeline has all the appearance of traditional shorthand. It is a 'free' system, giving in many cases a choice of outline to suit the individual writer, who does not need to learn the whole system in order to be able to make use of it.

My late husband, James Hill, preferred to say that he 'discovered' rather than 'invented' Teeline for, as a writer and teacher of an existing method, he never set out to invent another system of shorthand. This was partly because, following the invention and use of recording machines, it was widely predicted that the need for shorthand would diminish, and partly because he did not regard Teeline (or Boscript,[1] as it was first called) as anything but an intellectual exercise, indulged in as time allowed and brought out and demonstrated as the occasion demanded.

One such occasion was when he was called upon to teach sufficient shorthand to a group of trainee nurses to enable them to take notes of their nursing lectures. They attended college only for one year, one day a week and out of that day had only a couple of hours for shorthand instruction. Another was when he undertook to teach various colleagues during their lunch breaks enough shorthand for personal note-taking.

He had for more than twenty years been interested in all forms of shorthand and in the use of language generally, but his main preoccupation during that time had been to discover a better way of presenting shorthand theory so that more meaningful material could be introduced early in the learning process. He felt this would help to reduce the high drop-out rate in evening classes.

Research into word frequency applied to shorthand theory showed that, in order to give a wider vocabulary, the CON- and COM- prefixes, the -ING suffix, S, and a method for representing T and D would have to be taught early in the system. The only really surprising thing to come from this research was the high percentage of commonly used words that included T and D in their endings. From this work it eventually became clear that the essential characteristics of a good shorthand system were actually present in ordinary handwriting and that if only handwriting could be sufficiently streamlined, it would not be necessary to learn shorthand at all.

It is doubtful, however, since James Hill was engaged in full-time teaching, whether he would ever have developed Boscript fully had it not been for a series of events that occurred between May and December 1966.

First, he discovered that some of his less-able students could take dictation for short periods in handwriting (using known abbreviations) almost as fast as they could in shorthand. This led them to ask why they had wasted almost six months in trying to learn shorthand, and led him to consider seriously the possibility of teaching a fast writing system to those not capable of benefiting from traditional shorthand.

Secondly, on a visit to a local factory, he had been told that the main problem encountered by a work study team was their inability to write down quickly enough what they were observing. This had immediately triggered the suggestion that they should learn how to apply work study techniques to handwriting and that perhaps Boscript could be developed to meet this need.

Thirdly, he had been informed at the beginning of the summer vacation that in September, which was the start of a new academic year, he would have to teach shorthand to trainee journalists. This group, from various local papers, attended the college for only one day each week and spent 1 hour a week in learning shorthand. In two years this gave a maximum of 72 hours' instruction time, at the end of which they were expected to take a qualifying examination at 100 w.p.m. It was an impossible target to reach, so the decision was made to teach them Boscript.

Fourthly, a leaflet appeared on the college notice-board, announcing the formation of Heinemann Educational Books and inviting the submission of technical manuscripts to that company. James decided to send a summary of his note-taking system. Subsequently he was asked to produce a small booklet outlining the principles of the system to establish copyright and to test the possible demand for such a book.

In the months preceding this event, work had begun in earnest on the perfecting of Boscript and, because of the importance of the letter T and the fact that it had been one of the first letters to be used in its streamlined form, the name of the system was changed to Teeline. It is significant that the discoverer chose not to call it Hill's Shorthand, largely because he was self-effacing, and also because he said that if *he* had not discovered it, then someone else would have done so. It was simply there, waiting to be found. The amazing thing was that no one else had done so.

He also said that Isaac Pitman, living in the age of the steam locomotive and the pen, had invented a system as beautiful and complex as the former, and written with the latter. Teeline suited the age of the diesel and the ballpoint. James felt that if Pitman had lived in the twentieth century, he might well have discovered Teeline himself.

The first step in reducing ordinary writing had been to decide what letters could be omitted from words and still leave a recognizable 'skeleton'. Countless hours were spent on this task and the results analysed.

The second step, and one that took a great deal longer to complete to his satisfaction, was to reduce the movement required in the formation of the letters themselves. So far as could be measured, the application of these two principles reduced handwriting by about two-thirds. If this assessment was correct, then it ought to be possible to double or treble handwriting speed.

The third step was to discover at what speeds people normally write. Here, there was a wide range from about 24 w.p.m. at the lower end to around 45 at the upper end with, of course, a few people writing at less than 24 and more than 45. Taking 35 w.p.m. as an average speed, and applying the two Teeline principles outlined above, a potential speed of between 70 and 105 w.p.m. could be expected, once the response in Teeline had become as automatic as the handwriting response.

Teeline was described, therefore, as 'a new and exciting form of handwriting'. The term 'shorthand' was avoided, not only to stress the basic difference between Teeline and the existing methods, but also because of the psychological effect the term had on those who had already failed to learn one of the traditional systems.

A series of experimental courses justified the truth of his reasoning.

3

One of the journalists in the trainee group passed her qualifying 100 w.p.m. speed test in less than the two years allowed, and actually demonstrated the system at a Press conference in London in July 1968 at speeds up to and including 200 w.p.m. on unseen material. Her total tuition time had been about 35 hours spread over two terms, after which she had simply used Teeline in her daily work. She had received no real speed training as such.

Teeline proved excellent for evening and part-time day classes. Once-a-week 2-hour classes enabled a variety of students, including housewives and business people, to learn Teeline and reach speeds of 40, 50 and even 60 w.p.m. in 24–36 hours. Many took local speed examinations, which caused a certain amount of consternation among the Board's officials as the system was not recognized and there was no examiner for it; but there was no denying the high accuracy of the transcripts. From this came one of the early slogans – 'If you can write, you can write Teeline'. What is more, they could read what they had written.

Classes at Derby College of Further Education ran for 10 weeks, 2 hours a week, in which time the theory was completed. Twenty-six of the students elected to continue to attend for a further nine weeks and at the end of that time (38 hours) took regional speed examinations.

The results were: 40 w.p.m. Eight passed (five with distinction); 50 w.p.m. Fourteen passed (twelve with distinction); 60 w.p.m. Two passed (one with distinction). Only two of the twenty-six failed. In the report giving these results it was stated that other students at the same college usually required about 120 hours to take and pass the examination at those speeds.

Speeds achieved varied not so much according to the number of hours, but to the spread of learning. Longer courses gave more time for assimilation and speed-building.

An experimental course held in 1968 at Sheffield College of Technology for trainee journalists ran for 8 weeks, during which time James Hill travelled there three times a week from Nottingham to give 2-hour lessons. Allowing for time lost in enrolment and examination, the course lasted only 42 hours. The test, supervised by the shorthand consultant for the National Council for the Training of Journalists, consisted of five-minute passages and the results were passes by all eleven students at either 60 or 70 w.p.m. One of them gained 100 per cent accuracy in transcription, four had 99 per cent or over and no one had less than 95 per cent. These results were described as 'verging on the incredible'. Other learners would not have completed the theory in that time.

This course was followed by one at the offices of the Wolverhampton *Express and Star* when, after 56 hours' tuition, spread over 6 weeks, speeds of 50–80 w.p.m. were reached on the final three-minute test passages, no one gaining less than 97 per cent accuracy in transcription.

It is interesting to note that both these courses were taught before there was a textbook, a little blackboard instruction being followed by a lot of dictation and reading back from notes. The results of the courses led to Teeline being accepted as a suitable system for journalists to learn, with the added advantage that theory could be completed in less than half the time required for other systems. Speed-building could, therefore, start earlier.

Teeline took a long time to find acceptance in schools and colleges. It was used at first for the less-able students and on short courses such as part-time day and evening classes. Notable exceptions were Oxford College of Further Education, where in 1970–71 the French adaptation was pioneered (closely followed by a German adaptation), and the South Warwickshire College of Further Education. In 1971 both these colleges made the decision to teach only Teeline.

One of the advantages of Teeline was the ease with which it could be adapted to foreign languages and Belfast College of Business Studies later produced a Spanish Teeline course with tapes. World of Learning produced a programmed instruction course with tapes and Reach-a-Teacha Ltd followed with a taped instruction course for use with the textbook. Both these courses include some speed-building.

The system is now firmly established in the UK as one of the recommended systems, suitable for all types of courses, and there are now sufficient books to satisfy all needs.

Teeline found its way to New Zealand as long ago as 1968, when a journalist visiting England took back one of the first published books. Now, Teeline is widely taught all over that country. In Zimbabwe (then Rhodesia) Teeline was adopted for journalists at about the same time – 1969 – and the tradition is still being observed.

At the time of writing, the system has been introduced into Bahrain, Fiji, parts of Australia and Canada, Singapore and Denmark, where a Danish adaptation of the textbook has been printed. It is found easy to learn by those for whom English is a second language.

Although the system has been developed over the years, the fundamental theory has changed remarkably little.

The Teeline Association, a non-profit-making organization, begun in 1971 to link up the pioneers, produces a quarterly magazine giving news and advice to writers and teachers. It also runs a Proficiency Test for intending teachers and successful candidates receive a certificate.

Teeline Education Ltd, also formed in 1971 to promote the system, runs a round-the-year speed examination service for students, though this is in addition to those held by the Royal Society of Arts, the London Chamber of Commerce and Industry and other examining bodies. To date, the highest speed recorded in examinations is 150 w.p.m. for four minutes, but there are unofficial records of higher speeds being reached.

Unfortunately, the discoverer of Teeline died in June 1971, before he had fully completed his work, but each year more and more people learn his system and have reason to be grateful to him. The delight frequently expressed by them in discovering Teeline would have pleased him greatly. Little did he think when he began work on a method of fast writing for those who were not able for various reasons to master older shorthands, that Teeline would one day be accepted as a shorthand in its own right.

Nevertheless, teachers must not forget that, though it is as good as the traditional systems, it is not the same, for it is built on what is already known. It is, in short, only ordinary handwriting to which work study principles have been applied.

[1] *Editor's note:* Mrs I. C. Hill is known to her friends as 'Bo' and it was in honour of her that James Hill first called his system 'Boscript'.

Chapter 2 Teeline and the Teacher

MERIEL BOWERS

My introduction to Teeline came when George Hill, son of its founder, came to the college where I teach and gave a one-morning 'trip' through the system. What a whirl it was – and so was my head at the end of it! But, despite this, it was possible to see how quickly and easily the various shapes fell into a logical pattern, and I was quite impressed.

As the college was starting a new schools link-course, with fifth-year girls coming for five mornings a week for a 'commercial course' (typewriting, office practice and shorthand, aiming for CSE and any other external certificates they could accrue along the way), Teeline seemed tailor-made for the shorthand part of the course.

I taught myself from *Basic Teeline* during the summer holidays, getting very confused with the outlines in the supporting book (*Practice Exercises*) which used big D and interjoined vowels. I began teaching Teeline in the autumn term, not feeling very confident but at least making sure I was one jump ahead each day. An old maxim is 'the best way to learn shorthand is to teach it' and how true this still is! From these rather humble beginnings, plus an evening class the same year (composed mainly of drop-outs from other systems) I evolved a teaching plan which basically I still use, although the original notes have been altered as experience showed better ways of dealing with difficulties.

I worked on the premise that, unlike myself, students were not inhibited by another system of shorthand. Their learning problems were going to be quite different from the learning problems of those of us in the teaching profession who were already steeped in one or more other systems. Therefore, from the outset, one should forget dry-penning and three-line drilling of every exercise that comes along.

It will be found that practising teachers trained in another form of shorthand have most difficulty in *reading* printed Teeline, but students do not have this problem – once they get the idea of reading for context. Their main difficulty is penmanship and the first few lessons should be devoted to writing strokes, meaningful joinings and simple sentences. This will amply justify and repay the time spent so doing.

Make haste slowly over the first few hours, meanwhile training the students to use their notebooks to best advantage. Go round the room checking what and how the students are writing; bend over their desks to demonstrate how the shapes should be written to improve on their own efforts and then watch how the students imitate your strokes. Look out for one elementary difficulty in that while students may write H

7

downwards in response to your plea, they are not writing a following R (say), by sliding back up the stroke and then writing R upwards from the top of the H in what they think is the correct manner. The idea of reducing longhand words and then applying theory knowledge to build up the required outlines is a skill that is acquired very quickly.

A good way of dealing with the first lesson is to divide the alphabet into two halves with some writing practice on the first half before moving on to the second. Stress that vowels have two signs and make a repetitive game out of this. At the end of the lesson display on your chalkboard a sentence that the class can read for itself – something on the lines of 'Today we had a first lesson in Teeline and soon we shall be able to use it to take notes and build up a high speed'. What matter that the theory is not strictly correct? Motivation and interest are high and you have whetted their curiosity.

The Teeline should then be copied several times so that the rate of writing is about 50–60 w.p.m. which enforces the idea that writing at speed is what shorthand is all about. It is not the ability to read sentences from the board that is the ultimate aim, but to develop and build upon this skill so that the hand can fly across the pages of the notebook without conscious thought. Even by the end of the first lesson it will be observed, as one goes round the class, that the students are attempting to write their names in Teeline (plus friends' names as well) and I always encourage this student participation even though the outlines are very basic.

A short test is recommended at the end of every week with full-time students. I suggest a simple dictated test of, say, ten words on points of theory covered during the week, plus ten special forms and word groupings. Ask the student to number one to twenty down the page beforehand and then take in the page for marking. This is a revealing test, not only of student learning, but also of your own teaching, and is quickly given. It shows who has got problems and what form they take, and thus they can be dealt with in the next lesson. This is the only actual marking I do with beginners, but all the class time is spent with the students, advising and correcting throughout the lesson.

It is also a sound plan to have a summing-up session every week so that everything taught to date is analysed – what the student should know and what help is needed. If any students have been absent, appropriate homework can be set to enable them to catch up.

I do give three-line drills occasionally, mainly as consolidation, but the students work from their own shorthand copied from a book or the board, thus emphasizing the freedom and lack of rigidity of the system. By constantly moving among the students one can check that a reasonable facility is being developed, and after this some attempt should be made to teach the students to 'tidy up' their outlines.

Again, not losing sight of the free system aspect, nor of each individual's own handwriting style, some training is necessary in writing outlines fairly close together and not so large and cumbersome that they occupy the whole of the line space available. I have found that using a common word drill to start a lesson with the aim of getting all the words on one line is a useful way to practise. I use such words as *if*, *is*, *as*, *the*, *and*, etc., together with *you*, *your*, *we*, *very*, the latter filling a twofold purpose by emphasizing the difference in the U, Y, W, V shapes.

Students love the challenge of reading and occasionally writing sentences that have been written on the board in Teeline, but some need a great deal of encouragement in the art of reading for sense. They will ponder endlessly over one dubious outline and need teacher help to read on the next few words, or drawing 'skeletons', until realization dawns. It is heartwarming to see the whole class busy at this type of exercise, and a little healthy competition can be engendered by timing the first one to complete.

Teachers who know another shorthand as their primary system will find that sometimes they end up with a 'foreign' outline in the midst of their blackboard Teeline. Do not despair if this occurs because it happens to everyone and (as some slight consolation) it becomes less frequent as the years go by. Why not take the students into your confidence and make a game out of it? I used to draw a little 'hangman' figure at the side of the board every time I wrote a 'foreign' outline during the lesson. Human nature being what it is, students love to catch the teacher out, but the need for this prop eventually lessens, even though one might be dealing with two or even three shorthand systems during the same college session.

Handouts can be introduced written in Teeline with two blank lines which can be used initially as reading exercises, reading several times. The better students should succeed with the first attempt, the weaker students with subsequent ones. Afterwards the blank lines can be filled in by copying the teacher's shorthand from dictation.

If other members of staff are prepared to work as a team, several sets of handouts can be kept in readiness. Not only does this ease one teacher's work-load, it also gives the student an insight into other writing styles, reinforcing once again the freedom of the system: as long as the basic rules are obeyed, there is no right and wrong way – just a different way!

Which leads to the statement that my colleagues and I are agreed upon: that beginners need rules, with the freedom of the system being developed later. They need a good foundation on which to lay the basis for speed, and knowing the rules is a sure way of achieving it. A student needs to know that T followed by R or vowel-R is written as one movement, not two, so ensure that the basic rules are being observed in order to foster good habits from the start.

It is very limiting to insist that the student writes absolutely correct outlines. Who is to say which is the better outline for each individual if the basic rules are not infringed? Certainly at the beginning, the teacher can suggest what is acceptable and why FT is written with the loop below, and FD with the loop above, but apart from this type of example it all depends on which form the student personally finds easier to write. By all means let students practise the alternatives, then decide which suits them best – this is where the freedom comes in!

A variation on reading material may be given in the form of a series of questions, the student having to read the question and then write the answer in sentence-form in Teeline. Make the questions impersonal, but interesting, covering as many theory points as you can (e.g. 'What is your favourite sport?' illustrating R followed by T). Papers can be exchanged for checking the answers and correctness of the shorthand and this encourages keenness in developing a checking skill, as they all endeavour to prove their neighbour wrong. If desired, the papers can be collected by the teacher for looking at later.

Another device that students enjoy is a passage relating to a particular topic at the appropriate time of the year – St Valentine's Day, Easter or Hallowe'en. Newspaper articles and magazines are a good source for this and can be adapted to suit the level of learning. I find that passages about Hallowe'en are particularly popular because, allowing for a mid-September start, a simple dictation skill has been developed by the end of October. In addition to the interest aroused, it is an excellent way to liberalize and add to a student's general knowledge.

Simple groupings should be taught – if not from the first lesson, certainly from the second. This develops an awareness of what makes a grouping and how common words that are linked together in speech can be linked together in Teeline. Students should also be trained to 'think' in Teeline so that when they hear the words *we have* they immediately think *we av* and proceed to write the outline; *sum ing* for *something*, *tras* for *trans* or *I inc* for *I think* and so on. This simple mnemonic can be very helpful from an early stage.

I have found that it is important to be enthusiastic about Teeline from the outset. The enthusiasm rubs off on to the student, who sees shorthand as a challenge. A target should be set for a goal at the end of the first term initially, and then for the end of the course. Stress that during the first week they will see 40 w.p.m. as a speed that they will never achieve, but by the end of the term they will be laughing at themselves for thinking such a target was unobtainable. I make a practice of reserving one or two passages at 40 w.p.m. and re-reading them when the student is attempting 80 w.p.m. I read at 40 and note that the students have time to look up and around the room during dictation, then double the speed and finally read it again at 120 w.p.m. This time they write over the take at 40, which should have been well-nigh perfect. It is an excellent way of motivating students to higher goals.

In the first few weeks I go through the main theory fairly quickly and develop a writing skill of 50–60 w.p.m. This is followed by a quick revision, followed by the extras of the system – intersections and the less common blends and word beginnings and endings. These are dealt with by collecting together dictation passages that include the new theory and using them as teaching material. Sets of dictation passages like this amply repay the time spent in preparation and can be added to or discarded over the years.

Students enjoy suggesting possible outlines for words they have not met before. The possibilities are legion for some complex words and one should get a consensus of opinion from the class, which provides a welcome respite from concentrated writing and helps break up the lesson.

Once students are confident in their own ability to think up an outline out of the blue, only difficult words should be given for practice purposes before a speed take.

So far we have been thinking how easily and quickly the basic theory can be taught because of its low learning load. However, the progression from about 70 w.p.m. takes as long to achieve and with a similar time-lag as other systems. The students know the outlines and can recall them quickly when not under pressure, but the stimulus-response bond has not yet been fully developed – the co-ordination has not been achieved between ear, brain, hand and even eye which is essential before a skill can be said to be automatic. The only way the stimulus-response bond can be developed is by regular and frequent practice for a short time once or twice each day. It is up to students to work in their own time to build up speed. The teacher can help, coax and encourage but ultimately the responsibility for progressing from one speed to the next rests with the student.

Class work should be supplemented by home transcriptions, thus giving practice in transcribing from a 'cold' note. Teacher-prepared cassettes at varying speeds are a great asset. It is worth considering getting together your own cassette bank which can be added to as convenient and necessary. The more members of staff who participate in preparation, the more one's personal load is lightened in increasing the number of tapes in stock. What is more important, it gives a variety of voices for the student to hear. Both male and female voices should be used if possible and if no male member of staff is available, the female teacher should appeal to husbands and boyfriends for help.

Once a writing skill has been acquired, it is not detrimental to have occasional practice with irregular timing as it gives an insight into office-style dictation. If a copying machine is to hand students should be advised to bring their own blank cassettes so that their particular speed requirement can be dubbed on to it for practice at home or during a free period.

If students wish to borrow a college tape from the dictation bank, they should be trained to enter the loan in the book provided so that a check can be kept on its whereabouts, with the teacher spot-checking on the state of the stock at intervals.

Practice in transcription is essential. Transcription is a skill in itself and the need for paragraphing, grammar and sentence structure and, above all, spelling, should be emphasized, with an insistence that full stops should be inserted during dictation. Very often a student whose English ability is only mediocre can shine at the theory stage, only to be disappointed when attempting to transcribe, and this proves the need for aptitude testing before accepting a student on a shorthand course.

In the main, except for testing purposes, transcription should be done at home, not in the lesson. It has always been said that in a shorthand lesson one should write shorthand and not longhand, and this is true whatever the system used. Every minute must count. From time to time one needs to see a written transcript which has been done under supervision and to check the notes in case anything is going wrong. Most courses, nowadays, allow some time for typed transcription and this gives an opportunity for the teacher to get a fair idea of the capabilities of the student.

Advantages of the Teeline system are:

1. students are interested from the outset and motivation is high;

2. attendance does not decline. Theory load is light so there is no chance of 'finding the going hard' with no apparent end in sight;

3. even the weaker students see the logic of the system and can visualize obtainable goals in the not-too-distant future;

4. very rewarding to teacher and learner with results soon obvious;

5. ideal not only for speed high-flyers but as a note-taking device (there is more need for this kind of training in a technological age);

6. the student does not have the drudgery of having to remember a vast amount of theory and spend endless hours on 'drills';

7. interesting material can be dictated from the outset. Words of three or four syllables (*lawyer, manager, opportunity*) are commonplace after the alphabet has been dealt with, so a wide variety of learning material can be used;

8. there is no need for the student to change the usual style of handwriting or to remember about strokes being light or heavy. Any kind of writing instrument can be used, even a felt-tip pen.

Chapter 3 Teaching the Early Lessons

DIANA AIREY

Every class you meet will know, from hearsay, what learning shorthand involves. The overall impression is that it is hard work involving lots of very difficult techniques. Students will have been made apprehensive by the myth.

If, in the first lesson, you can allay these fears by emphasizing the flexibility of Teeline, by stressing that all they have to do is to learn how to read back their own version, that there is no 'right' or 'wrong' outline, you will have set the scene for light-hearted, relaxed classes. And, indeed, why not!

Teaching should be about capturing the imagination of students, motivating them to acquire new knowledge, or develop a new skill. In Teeline, as in other subjects where the reaction between thought processes and movement needs to become almost instantaneous, a student who is enjoying the lesson benefits greatly from the reduction of tension.

Such tension often results from the attempt simultaneously to listen, retain and write outlines that have not easily registered in the mind; therefore the aim should always be to give instruction in a manner that assists easy absorption and retention. Make it fun and you'll usually make it stick! It is a problem, in any case, to explain the free and easy system of Teeline. There are no rules as such, no boundaries, no confines. No outline is absolutely wrong. There are better, faster, clearer ways of writing a word, but only if it suits the writer.

This message, however, can be counter-productive in the early stages. People are used to rules and regulations, and there is comfort or security in obeying them. We have been taught the difference between right and wrong since we were in high chairs and first threw porridge at the dog. A certain smug satisfaction comes from being right. And yet, in comes the Teeline teacher repeatedly saying 'It doesn't matter'. It *does* matter to them and reassurance is needed until the class understands why it does not matter.

Of course there are guide-lines. Some outlines are more economical if written in a certain way. Some outlines may be easier for some people to transcribe. But we all have our own style of handwriting, and so we all have our own style of writing Teeline.

The criterion is: can you read back what you have written? If the answer is yes, then do not interfere; you have taught them to *know* what they are doing, and that matters.

The first few lessons will be the foundation stones for the rest of the course. Once the class know the guide-lines upon which the system is based, and the Teeline alphabet as thoroughly as they know the longhand one, all the other contractions and refinements will be logical and easy. Constantly recap, revise and reinforce the first few steps. This not only has the advantage of a good grounding, but ensures that the slow starters, and the students who miss a class in these important early stages, do not get left behind.

To demonstrate how Teeline works, write two or three connected sentences on the board:

Cn u rd ths?
Mry hd a ltl lm.
Old King Cl ws a mry old sl.
Onc upn a tm.

By asking the class some leading questions and by dropping heavy hints, *they* will tell *you* what the guide-lines are, which you can then write on the board.

'Why were you able to read it – was there a connection?' you ask, and when they have found the answer, you write on the board: **Context**. Next you ask: 'What is missing from these sentences? Are all the vowels omitted?' On the board, you write: **Omit vowels – except at beginning of word**. (You can choose whether or not to explain that vowels can also be included at the end of words if preferred – or if sounded: e.g. *radio, camera*. You may prefer to leave this refinement to a later lesson.) 'Have any other letters apart from vowels been omitted?': **Use only one of the doubled letters**. 'Is there anything unusual about the word *lamb*?': **omit silent letters**. 'Here are two words taken from those rhymes but written differently. What are they?' You then put on the board: Kl (*cole*), Wns (*once*) and the answer: **Spelling**.

There are many examples available to emphasize the concept of Teeline using skeleton longhand. Several themes can be used such as proverbs, song titles, football teams or the names of the class members, but beware of obscurity. Writing song titles popular in the 1950s may mean very little to a group who were born in the 1960s.

Teeline is based heavily on spelling, so we are able to use knowledge already acquired and not something new. According to experts, and unbeknown to us, when we hear a word like *college* a sort of ticker-tape runs behind the eyes and we 'see' the word as it is spelt and not as it is heard – 'kolej'. Some students find it difficult to isolate the consonants quickly, so it may be necessary to give plenty of practice in reading and writing skeleton words and paragraphs before tackling the Teeline alphabet.

If the class can read fluently a passage written in longhand within the framework of the guide-lines used in Teeline, this will be a step towards gaining confidence when transcribing shorthand notes.

So happily to the Teeline alphabet. The alphabet is based on the longhand one but it is necessary to revert to the cursive, copperplate style of writing some of the letters. Examples of these pretty letters can be seen in old bills or church registers and often older friends or relatives of the class still write an F with the lazy daisy petal shape, or an S with a little hole in it. You may prefer to demonstrate the consonants including TH, CH, WH and SH first, introducing the vowels separately afterwards. This will certainly help to eliminate some confusion as to why most vowels have two symbols. Whichever method you favour, emphasize that it is the *indicator* that is used for an outline beginning with a vowel. Although this is not always the case (A before an R, for example) it will be less confusing if this point is saved for a later lesson.

It is important that R is written from the line up, but it does not matter if the Q slopes one way or the other. The relative sizes and positions of letters can be linked to the longhand letters. M is as high and as wide as the longhand one, P and H are only the 'stick' of the longhand letters, but set in the same place. The hairpin Q is evolved from writing QU joined together. There is an obvious economy of movement when a B is written all in one fell swoop, but is the same size as the lower case B.

The exact positions of the letters seem to be all important to beginners but do try to reduce their tendency toward adopting such rigidity or they will feel uncomfortable later on when writing words like *put* and *pod*, *had* and *hit*.

Always seek to prepare the way for flexibility, and although the T *can* be written where the bar of the longhand T is positioned, it will be quicker if they keep the pen on the paper. Leave the disjoining technique for the word endings.

Linking the longhand words to the alphabet also has a logic. B says *be*, R says *are*. We already use N for *and* in longhand as in *fish 'n' chips* or *cash 'n' carry*. When the initials V.G. and V.I.P. appear, we know that the V means *very*, and there used to be road signs bearing a large black cross which meant *accident* black spot. Relating these words to the letters gives plenty of opportunity for demonstrating yet again how the letters are written.

Your students will copy the way you write P and H downwards and an R upwards. The most important visual aid you have is yourself. With a piece of chalk and a blackboard, show them how it is done and then dictate the alphabet so that they can write it. It is worth while dictating the alphabet followed by the sounds of SH, WH, CH and TH (taking care to pronounce the SH as if telling a child to be quiet) backwards, forwards and out of sequence until everyone can read and write without hesitation. Dictate the related words, too: i.e. *able, a, at, be, c, do/day,*

15

electric etc., until the class can confidently write the outline which is for both the letter and the word at random.

Dictation at the earliest possible stage is most important. Copying is all very well, but dictation encourages the group to write from the spoken word. This, as well as getting them acclimatized to your dulcet tones, allows each student to maintain their own individual style of writing. It is a bit arrogant, as well as nonsensical, to say that Teeline is based on longhand and then only to allow the class to write in the style of your own longhand. You may disapprove of 'backward' writing; you may prefer to take notes in pencil; you may love the upward L and the hook N in the blend WN. Fine, that is your prerogative. But your pleasure must come not from being 'right', but in the accuracy of the transcription which will surely come back to you from the students.

After you have taught the alphabet with the words that go with it, try writing in Teeline on the board *He will go today* or *She will go to the ball* or *From me to you* and somebody will read it back. Added excitement can be generated by actually dictating several short simple sentences and then asking individual members of the class to read them back to you. Thus not only have they recognized your outlines, but are beginning to recognize their own. They are also given the opportunity to develop their own style of joining the letters without being inhibited by the confines of your style and that of the textbook. There will be plenty of time in future lessons to demonstrate the efficacy of faster, clearer ways of writing.

Here are some examples of sentences I have used and clearly you will be able to think of many more:

It was a very hot day, so we had a swim.
The hen had laid two eggs.
The cabbage was big and fed all of them.
It was kind of you to visit me.
The girl had an accident in her car.

However banal the sentences might be, the pleasure and satisfaction your class will get from being able to read back the 'dreaded' shorthand so early in the course will encourage all of you.

Remember, you scrabblers at the chalk face of education, the alphabet letters are your foundation stones. Lay them well, and they will last a lifetime.

Chapter 4 Converting to Teeline with a Sixth Form

PAULINE HOSKING

I had been interested in Teeline for some years and toying with the idea of teaching it to the sixth form. Early in 1981, it became clear that in September the Business Studies Department would need to provide for a student intake of a much wider level of ability and attainment and, probably, with less time at our disposal. The time seemed ripe to introduce Teeline.

The sixth form has a large proportion of students for whom English is their second language, and we were expecting a group consisting of some students taking one or two A levels, some resitting O levels, some hopefully converting CSE subjects to O levels, and some taking special English proficiency examinations. I decided to try out Teeline with one mixed group, to see what the result would be; we had one lesson of Teeline for 1 hour per day.

All levels of ability took to the Teeline alphabet like the proverbial ducks to water. There was no lack of comprehension; I did not have to hunt around for different ways of explaining theory so that *everyone* understood. We were using the manuscript of *Teeline Shorthand Made Simple* made available to us by the author, Harry Butler. The system is so clear, so flexible and so easy to learn that there were no problems and everyone had a lot of fun (me included!). I had told the class that I had been a writer of another system for forty years (well, I didn't tell them exactly how many!) and that I had taught the system for nearly as long (thirty years). I also told them that they would have to keep their eyes open, because I was sure to make mistakes. They did (and I did). They enjoyed that! They had no difficulty in learning the special forms; I was slower to learn but they steered me gently along.

We spent the first two lessons (1 hour each) in giving time to the idea of Teeline spelling; then 3 separate hours on the Teeline alphabet, incorporating the special forms relevant to each letter of the alphabet. The next hour covered the vowel indicators, one at a time, with plenty of practice at each step. The following hour stressed the importance of first and last sounded vowels and the practice included plenty of special forms.

This brought us to the middle of the second week and the remaining 3 hours of that week were used to consolidate the basic alphabet, the use of the vowel indicators and the special forms. This may seem a long time (10 hours) but I have found with students of this age that all the time spent on the groundwork is time very well spent.

17

They could now write at a comfortable 40 w.p.m. – and for some it was too slow, so I gave repeats at 50 and 60. From then on, I gradually gave them the blends and prefixes and suffixes, which enabled them to shorten outlines, and they used them if they wished to do so. They found these of varying appeal – some they liked, others they forgot to use; some students were determined enough to practise the ones they found more difficult. A few gobbled up the lot and used them freely. Again, one of the beauties of the system is that students do not *have* to use the blends – they can write Teeline without them – but if they can use these shortening devices, speed improves rapidly.

From the beginning of this phase to the end, we constantly revised each device as it occurred, the students comparing their outlines. By Christmas, they were writing repetitions easily at 40/50/60 w.p.m. By April, most could take and transcribe 50/60 on new matter and one or two managed 80.

I know that some students found Teeline so easy that they were inclined to skip their homework and another year I shall be much firmer about this. The result of their over-confidence (or laziness) showed later, and the lazy ones were those who could not take more than 70, with any hope of transcribing accurately, by May. Some, of course, were not lazy, but their difficulties were with the English language rather than with Teeline.

By the end of April, I had given an examination paper of speeds of 70, 80, 90 and 100 w.p.m. for transcription, the students choosing one of these speeds to transcribe. (There were good transcriptions at each of these speeds.) This had never been possible with other systems at this point in the course.

From here on it is, as with any system, the hard grind of speed-building; but because we could discuss and compare all the alternative outlines, it was easier to maintain a higher level of interest and motivation with Teeline.

After learning the basic alphabet (and one of the joys of the system is that in such a short time they can write anything!) we had fascinating sessions where the girls did the blackboard work (I'm not stupid!) and compared their outlines. Some were very clever forms; this gave them great satisfaction.

From the beginning, I found that they could read back quite difficult matter with comparative ease. Their transcription was quicker and more accurate than the non-Teeline groups' transcription. I think of shorthand as a form of 'applied English' and where the student has a low English ability/experience and a small vocabulary (and some of our students are still *learning* to speak the language) there are the usual difficulties with unfamiliar words. One example (and, of course, this kind of thing applies to audio-typewriting, too) is *hard wear* typed back as *hardware* (they seem to be familiar with the shop!).

The totally unfamiliar words cannot be recognized or understood and therefore they cannot find them in a dictionary. Although Teeline does give a lot of help in reading back, it cannot perform miracles. So two members of the class who had great problems with English (one a Chinese girl who, because of her special way of pronouncing English words, had a particular difficulty) were not ready to take a May examination, yet had enjoyed their Teeline work.

The rest of the group took their Stage I RSA Shorthand examination in May. This was unusual; we do not often manage that – not for more than a handful. All the students passed except for one – one at 50 w.p.m. and the rest at 60.

The results from Teeline were impressive with students able to reach examination standard more quickly and less painfully than other groups. The change-over to Teeline for me was much easier than I had feared.

Chapter 5 Teaching Mixed-Ability Groups

PEGGY BLACKHURST

Teeline is fun! Teeline is easy to learn! Teeline gives you something that the others have not got!

This is the approach that I found worked like a charm with mixed-ability groups in bilateral and, later, in comprehensive schools. When the skills subjects of shorthand and typewriting have been included in a school's curriculum, they have to justify their existence. As a result, pupils who would not be accepted in further education classes because of lack of qualification are given the option of taking these subjects.

While most shorthand teachers in schools would like students to have a certain amount of ability in English, particularly as regards spelling and grammar, this is not always possible. Teachers of other subjects have to accept a wide range of ability so they see no reason why the shorthand teacher should not do likewise. Of course, 'streaming' or 'setting' can be carried out in these other subjects, but all too often the shorthand teacher finds that this is not possible. Usually the O level pupils are creamed off and the shorthand class has only pupils of that standard when shorthand does not clash in the options with a required O level. This is reasonable as secretarial subjects with O levels is preferable, but it limits the shorthand department, which may be reduced to only one class of very mixed ability, and rarely more than three classes.

So the position at the beginning of the school year is that pupils have opted for shorthand for three reasons:

1. they want to work in an office and think that shorthand will help them to get a good job;
2. they do not like the other options offered and decide that the one they know nothing about must be better than the ones they have already tried;
3. shorthand is 'grown-up'.

The first group pose very little problem as they are motivated. The other two come along ready (and apparently enthusiastically) to 'give it a whirl' – some who are downright lazy and see the subject as an easy option, and others who try hard but are lacking in ability and whose thinking is a slow process. This is where the teacher first of all emphasizes the *fun* of acquiring a skill, which is still looked upon almost as a mystery by those who do not write shorthand.

The first groups arrive, all starry-eyed. They are given a short talk on how lucky they are that they are going to learn Teeline – for the three reasons given at the beginning of this chapter. They are then divided into groups, which will all be of mixed ability, because there is no really satisfactory way of grading them at this point. Later they can be graded according to speed. The English teacher can be of some help here, but it does not always follow that English ability reflects Teeline ability. Speed of mind and speed of hand play a much bigger part than an English teacher realizes.

The first lesson begins with the handing out of notebooks and textbooks. There is already a small glow of pride because this notebook is just like the ones real reporters use. Show them how to rule a margin quickly without the aid of a ruler, how to flip pages over. Tell them that a page must be dated with each new piece of work – and ask them why. You will probably be surprised to find how many of them know this.

Treat them immediately as if they are trainee reporters and they will respond to this – most of them want to leave school and consider themselves 'grown-up'. Show them how to sit properly and how to hold their pencils or pens correctly.

Now for the Teeline. Tell them they are going to love Teeline. It's fun, it's easy, it's a secret language that not everyone can read. Tell them that anyone who can write, can write Teeline. Ask them if anyone present cannot write, and praise them because they all can. They know this is a mild joke and their smiles may be a little pitying, but the tone has been set. They are going to enjoy Teeline and they are going to be successful.

Next, tell them that Teeline is an abbreviation of what they already know. Ask them to see if they can read what you are about to write on the board. Write: *U r v lcky ppl bcs u r gng to lrn Tln.* According to the type of pupil, they will either be saying this aloud as you write, or you will have to ask who can read it. You can be sure that someone will manage to do so. Praise them again – this is most important, as nothing succeeds like success, and the desire to be praised is very strong in teenage children. (Never believe a teenager who says 'I don't care'. This teenager cares most deeply.)

Now write: *U r v clvr to b abl to rd tht sntnc so qkly. U r rdy to lrn th Tln alphbt.* Let them read this to you. Explain that they now know the basic principle of Teeline – abbreviation. Tell them that James Hill started this way and then thought that if the words could be abbreviated, so could the letters.

Write the alphabet on the board, taking a letter at a time, explaining how each is formed and emphasizing the smallness of the vowels. Ask them how they think the letter will be written before you put it on the board. By the time you get to K they will be getting the idea. Point out that legible Teeline is preferable to badly written outlines, just as legible longhand is essential.

Do not worry if you do not complete the alphabet in this lesson – work right up to the bell for the next lesson. Let them see how disappointed you are that the lesson is over; tell them to practise and learn what they have already written and read the first part of their textbooks. The following lessons should be taught with this same emphasis on enjoyment and praise for success.

Do not linger too long on each new principle. Get through the textbook as quickly as possible, and revise each principle in turn at the beginning of the following speed lessons. Set exercises from the textbook for homework – mostly transcription exercises. Make use of gimmicks. For example, a portrait of a pupil can be drawn using the Teeline for the pupil's name and then adding the rest of the face; or the outline for *train* can be turned into a locomotive by adding a few lines and circles for wheels. Keep the lessons varied and interesting, but keep to a weekly pattern as regards transcription and examination days.

Do not neglect transcription lessons. Have one a week, preferably for typed transcription, because many pupils can read their outlines but cannot make sense of them if their English is poor.

Spend part of every lesson in dictation, taken from a previous chapter, or from one of the Teeline workbooks. Always have the dictation read back. Keep a record before you of who has read back in past lessons so that every pupil has a turn at this. Mixed-ability classes do not like one or two pupils always shining and, despite apparent reticence, like to read back.

Play the game of 'Tell her/him!' That is, if a pupil cannot read an outline after you have mentally counted five, you say 'Tell her/him!' to the class. This prevents the reading back being held up and the class getting bored. If you think one person's attention is wandering, ask that person to 'Tell her/him'. Another ploy is to get the rest of the class to write over their outlines while the pupil is reading back, trying to keep up with the reader but never going ahead. They can write many times over an outline which is causing the reader difficulty. You can then ask who managed to write some very black outlines – and praise them if they do.

When the theory has been studied and speed-building takes priority, 'set' groups according to speed if there is more than one class, but be flexible in moving students up or down as they progress. Whether you have one group or more, you will find that students write at different speeds. Now is the time to introduce tapes, so that any fast students are not held back.

A weekly test under examination conditions is very helpful, as these mixed-ability classes usually contain a high proportion of students who are very nervous of examinations. By doing this, you will help to reduce examination nerves.

Students should be enjoying their Teeline now, but still keep up the 'fun'. If you have any drawing ability, make colourful charts of the alphabet. I have used an alphabet chart, dotted with 'humanized' mice, on which Teeline outlines were superimposed. The same idea can be used for speed charts where a pupil's speed (under examination conditions) is recorded, for example, by mice climbing an ear of corn, each grain having a speed – the possibilities are endless. If you are not artistic, cut out pieces from wrapping paper to make up your chart. This idea may seem childish but pupils love it, even the most mature of them. Make sure that all the pupils manage to get their names on the chart before the course is over. I have never known anyone unable to achieve 40 w.p.m. in two passages out of three at two minutes each.

At the end of the course, whether the pupils will make shorthand writers or not, all will have improved their English, spelling, punctuation and comprehension. What is perhaps as important is that they will have recognized the need for good English. They will have acquired a new interest in language that would not have been accepted in any other way. They have been learning English from the day they went to school; to them it is the 'same old stuff' but Teeline, with its enjoyment and promise of success, has widened their horizons. I taught English for many years and have rejoiced in the opportunity to teach it painlessly through Teeline.

Chapter 6 Block Release and Day Release Courses

PAUL BERRY

Teaching Teeline for twelve years to block and day release students at Kingsway-Princeton College, London, was rewarding and enjoyable.

With the occasional exception, block and day release students are strongly motivated, although sometimes students will admit that they have been persuaded to obtain a secretarial qualification as 'something to fall back on'. The majority of students, however, have consciously chosen a secretarial career and are eager to make the most of the opportunity of being released by their employer for training, either for one day a week, or, for the more fortunate block course students, on a full-time basis.

Block course participants are school-leavers of from 16–18 years of age. They are selected by employers after interview and test, and hopefully most of them will have obtained an English language pass, either at O level or CSE Grade 1, in the June examinations. They attend college for 22–24 weeks during the autumn and spring terms.

Teeline, typewriting and transcription training constitute the core subjects of the block course timetable, but with the emergence of the word processor and other office technology the curriculum has been augmented by a wide range of subjects reflecting the importance in all secretarial employment of a broad base of communication skills. In addition, the timetable is structured to allow approximately 3–4 hours a week of varied recreational activity. These classes provide a necessary relaxation from concentrated skill learning and also enable the students to mix with those on other courses and from other departments in the college.

Day release training is inevitably less broadly based. Some students attend classes for one whole day a week, but others for a morning or afternoon only. Their training consists of shorthand and typewriting, or, preferably, shorthand and typewritten transcription training if the students possess the necessary typewriting ability.

The goal for both block and day release students is identical: the ability to take dictation at an employable speed and to produce confidently and quickly a correct and accurately typed transcription. Defining 'an employable speed' always provokes a furore of controversy and a dozen different opinions, but after twenty-five years of teaching I believe the most practical criterion to be 80–100 w.p.m. shorthand at RSA standard with a typed transcription. Supporting this opinion is the fact that many employers with large secretarial staffs have salary schemes providing proficiency payments for RSA passes at these speeds, but do not recognize certificates from other examining bodies.

With a similar objective, the training of both block and day release students is fundamentally the same. One never ceases to wonder at the inexhaustible individuality of every new class, and although the basic Teeline teaching is constant, the pace and intensity of a course must always be measured to fit the ability, aptitude and application of the students.

Teaching the core subjects of Teeline, transcription training and typewriting is always closely interrelated. On block courses, three, sometimes four, and occasionally five members of staff are involved, and this requires constant collaboration and consultation. With day release classes only one or two teachers are needed.

Some staff resist group teaching, but it has many advantages. At Kingsway-Princeton it proved a most successful arrangement, with the students benefiting from different styles of presentation, a variety of teaching techniques, and from a change of teacher.

Block course students were entered for the RSA Shorthand-Typewriting Stage II examination at the end of their training, and the Teeline and typewritten transcription classes were especially closely dovetailed. The typewriting teachers participated by providing instruction and practice in the display of letters, memoranda, minutes, reports and other documents, but as the students were entered also for the RSA typewriting examinations it was necessary to devote an appreciable amount of time to these syllabuses.

The shorthand training revolved around the combination of two distinct but interlinking skills. The Teeline classwork was aimed primarily at achieving a speed of 100 w.p.m., while the transcription training built up brick by brick the ability to turn out accurate and quickly produced transcriptions.

Teeline training was based on three fundamental precepts. First, the importance of a very thorough understanding of Teeline theory, and the ability to apply that knowledge to new words as they occurred. Secondly, an insistence on neat and accurately written shorthand. Thirdly, on writing from dictation from the first lesson. I will deal in detail with these three points.

Teeline theory

Teeline has a lighter learning load than other shorthand systems, but of greater importance is the fact that, being an orthographic method, the principles are immediately comprehensible and easily assimilated. This has the inestimable advantage of enabling the theory to be learned thoroughly and in depth. My experience is that the best results are obtained by dividing a theory lesson into two parts.

Before giving a lesson dealing with the word ending -NCE, for example, a brief, simple passage was dictated containing two, or perhaps three, -NCE words, making sure that the outlines for all the other words were well known and easily written. After the dictation students were asked if there were any outlines they would like to check and the -NCE words duly emerged. These were written in longhand on the blackboard and the students quickly discovered deductively the new word ending. This was followed with 15–20 Teeline examples of the -NCE ending, choosing short, frequently used, and easily written examples, e.g. *chance, dance, France, distance, balance*, etc.

It is preferable for students to assimilate new outlines in a connected passage, and it was a simple matter to dictate short sentences including one of the new outlines. Whenever possible as many sentences were dictated as there were students so that they were all called upon to read back individually. Time permitting, the sentences were dictated again, but to keep students on the *qui vive* they were read in a different order, a word was added or omitted, or a sentence in the singular was rephrased in the plural.

This lesson was followed with longer and less frequently used words illustrating the same principle, e.g. *disturbance, experience, influence, announce, acceptance*, etc. The one-new-outline-in-a-sentence format was either repeated, or, to ring the changes, these longer words were included in a connected passage, together with some of the examples from the first batch, with which the students were by now familiar.

It is highly desirable to present the Teeline theory in the most systematic sequence possible, and after the -NCE word ending lesson students quickly grasp the logical progression to words ending in -NCY, such as *agency, tendency, emergency, proficiency, fluency*, etc. There are not many words in this group but some are long, and others occur infrequently, and it is a lesson that can be profitably repeated and reinforced at the speed-building stage.

A thorough Teeline grounding along the lines indicated has been the key to success in both block and day release training. Conversely, if students are pushed through the theory stage at a breakneck pace, speed-development training is a laborious, disheartening and painful business.

Legible shorthand

A twofold reward is to be reaped from an insistence on neat and accurate Teeline, with outlines written close together to minimize hand movement and to make maximum use of the notebook page. First, students take a greater pride in their work, and apply themselves more diligently. Secondly, well-written shorthand, like legible handwriting, is easier to read, and if the skeletal letters of a word are immediately recognizable transcription is faster and more certain. This discipline is particularly valuable with students whose slapdash inclinations tend to produce badly written, illegible shorthand.

From time to time we all have students whose transcription ability is weak, and this usually stems from poor and inaccurate shorthand. When one attempts to help such students one frequently meets the defensive response, 'Don't worry about my shorthand. I know it's bad but I can read it.' The simple truth is that not only is it bad, but that neither they nor anyone else could read it! Eradicating bad habits is a tortuous and time-consuming business, and it is a hundred times better to insist on well-written shorthand from the beginning.

Homework is an integral part of both block and day release training. During the theory and slow-speed training period this often consisted of transcribing a slowly dictated passage, or a Teeline exercise, and at the same time making a fair copy of the shorthand. The main mark was for an accurate transcription, but it was evident that students also valued the mark out of ten and the teacher's comments on the neatness, accuracy and style of the shorthand.

Early dictation

The third fundamental element of block and day release training was that from the outset dictation played a prominent part in every lesson. Almost without exception shorthand is used to record the spoken word, and it is essential that students become accustomed to taking dictation at the beginning of their training. Teeline scores heavily here as it is possible to build up quickly a substantial and rapidly increasing vocabulary of shorthand outlines.

To introduce diversity of activity, and to vary the tempo of the lesson, reading and copying printed Teeline, special form tests, word grouping drills – but only very occasionally putting longhand into Teeline – are useful and necessary adjuncts. Reading printed shorthand is particularly beneficial. As well as gaining confidence and fluency, students profit from the example of well-written outlines.

In the final analysis students are judged by their ability to record and transcribe the spoken word, and all block and day release training was specifically geared to this paramount objective.

Block course students are entered for a variety of RSA examinations in March at the end of their course, and, to acclimatize them to the special nerve-racking nature of shorthand examinations, all the students are entered for the London Chamber of Commerce and Industry 50 w.p.m. examination in the preceding November. There is always the student who could have attempted a higher speed but as it is only an interim assessment the examination is confined to 50 w.p.m.

In my last year at Kingsway-Princeton, after nine weeks of about 90 hours' tuition, out of a block release group of seventeen non-academic school leavers who took this LCCI examination, fourteen passed, nine with distinction. Two students in the group were awarded first and second places in the United Kingdom.

Transcription training

It has been said that one could teach a monkey to type, even if the result was to produce only balderdash. Learning shorthand is a major task, and training students to transcribe accurately is the other half of the battle.

The majority of block and day release students have minimal academic qualifications, and their transcription difficulties fall broadly into three separate categories: 1. basic weaknesses in English; 2. a lack of experience and general knowledge. This resulted at times in a hazy and incomplete understanding of the material dictated. On one occasion a student expostulated with me that it was very difficult to grasp the meaning of a passage which dealt with plants and machinery in the same breath! 3. a reluctance and/or inability to check and proof-read the work produced.

I believe that helping students to achieve an employable transcription standard is one of the most challenging and satisfying aspects of both block and day release teaching.

Training began with a few short, simple sentences immediately the students had mastered the typewriter keyboard. Before transcribing, the sentences were read back individually, and checked by cross-questioning to ensure correct spelling, punctuation, capitalization, etc. At the same time the rest of the group annotated their shorthand note to facilitate an accurate transcription.

The weak points in transcribing mentioned in 1. were dealt with in depth in individual lessons. Spelling was a perennial problem and overcoming this handicap was a non-stop struggle demanding patience and perceptive lesson preparation. It is easier to tackle commonly misspelt words such as *receive, separate, accommodation, occurred, recommendation, fulfil,* etc., than to anticipate the unexpected flood of idiosyncratic errors like *payed, consern, thier, lable, littel, check* for *cheque,* etc.

The possession of a dictionary was compulsory, and students were cajoled, coerced and good-naturedly chided into checking the spelling of every word about which they had any doubt. It is always hard to put a finger on one's own errors, and often students looked with a blind eye for their own mistakes – or had too much faith in their own infallibility! The use of dictionaries is permitted in RSA shorthand and typewriting examinations. With tongue in cheek, students were told that five marks were deducted for every spelling error, and to drive the point home five marks were deducted for spelling mistakes in all classroom work. The stratagem worked, and before long students became adept at avoiding the spelling traps, and developed a pride in producing acceptable transcriptions.

Plugging the gaps in general knowledge was a protracted task. Throughout the course as much help as possible was given by encouraging students to question any word or expression, or the tenor of a passage, which they did not understand, and by discussing and clarifying passages before dictating. It was also helpful to select material dealing with a particular commercial topic, such as banking, and to explain the specialized terms that occurred. At Kingsway-Princeton our block courses contained a nucleus of students from one of the leading banks and it was clearly beneficial for them to understand the terms current and deposit accounts, overdrafts, the drawer of a cheque, credit facilities, and so on. As most of the other students had just opened their first bank account the lesson was also relevant to them.

The mystery of the apostrophe was perhaps the nadir of the students' difficulties. There was much ribald laughter when at one block course team meeting I mentioned ruefully that my particular group of twenty-two girls hadn't an apostrophe between them!

There may well come a day when the apostrophe is consigned to oblivion, but until that time it is essential that secretaries and shorthand-typists know how, why and when to use it. I never cease to wonder that so many students from a wide range of schools emerge after five years of general education almost totally ignorant about the use of the apostrophe.

The first step was to clear the ground of words where an apostrophe indicated a missing letter as in *I'm, we'll, can't, o'clock*, etc. The heart of the matter was the use of the apostrophe to denote possession, and here it was necessary to progress slowly and carefully from simple examples, such as 'Jane's boyfriend', to nouns having a singular ending in 's' and sentences like 'James's girlfriend', 'Doris's new car', etc.

The greatest trials came with the difficult concept of 'the companies' accounts' or 'the company's accounts', and in expressions of time such as 'last year's examination results', 'next week's meeting', etc.

There were always one or two students who found the apostrophe an almost insoluble mystery. In desperation they scattered them wildly whenever a word ended with 's', and it was necessary sometimes to give individual tuition during the lunch hour.

Another successful activity was to give students a page from a daily newspaper and tell them to circle boldly all the apostrophed words they could find. Individual students were then called upon to write one or two examples on the blackboard and to explain to the class why an apostrophe was needed.

The class rule that students should always check their own work required constant emphasis. Effective proof-reading is an art acquired only with practice, demanding painstaking attention to detail, and the application of intelligence and common sense. On one occasion, endeavouring to drive home the distinguishing Teeline outlines for *production* and *protection*, I dictated a passage I had composed about the production of a government report on child protection. Amid a gale of hilarity five students handed in transcriptions about a government report on child production!

Two ploys noticeably improved the students' proof-reading ability. First, before any work was handed in for marking it had to be endorsed 'checked' and initialled, and this placed an inescapable onus on the student to proof-read every piece of work. Well-corrected errors were not penalized; one mark was deducted for each identified but uncorrected mistake, and three marks for an undetected error. Secondly, a set piece of work was collected from all students, with their names on the reverse side. These were then given out at random and students corrected each other's work. They did this with great zeal, and it certainly improved their ability to spot their own mistakes.

At the end of the block release courses in March, students were entered for the RSA 60, 80 and 100 w.p.m. shorthand examinations, as well as for the Shorthand-Typewriting Stage II certificate. In all shorthand classes there is a divergence of ability, but invariably all students passed at 60 w.p.m., and the majority at 80 w.p.m. The number passing at 100 w.p.m. varied from year to year depending upon the calibre of students, but usually about half were successful.

The volume of work to be accomplished in the Shorthand-Typewriting Stage II examination proved an arduous hurdle. Taking down and transcribing 800 words at 80 w.p.m., plus the additional tasks of composing a letter from dictated notes, and a manuscript tabulation, proved a little beyond the ability of many of the students. The pass rate fluctuated between approximately 30 and 40 per cent, but there is no doubt that this training provided probably the most valuable and realistic part of the course.

Day release students were entered for RSA examinations commensurate with their ability at the end of their year's course in June. The results depended to a large extent on the calibre, application and attendance of the student, but with both block and day release classes the examination results of those learning Teeline were better than I had been able to achieve with any other shorthand system.

I believe this to be the result of three factors:

1. The 'skeleton' of a word as represented by Teeline symbols is easily identified, and this complements the widely used 'look and say' method of teaching reading in the early learning stages.
2. Unlike phonetic systems of shorthand, Teeline requires no arduous vowel learning input. The five Teeline vowels A, E, I, O and U are derived from their alphabetical counterparts, and are easily recognized.

In addition, using these vowels initially and finally when they are pronounced is a very valuable aid to quick and accurate transcription.
3. Teeline is basically an orthographic shorthand system. The spelling of words is constantly emphasized and this has a very beneficial spin-off in helping students to produce acceptable transcriptions.

Teeline fulfils the fundamental educational precept of proceeding from the known to the unknown, and this plays a major part in creating in the classroom a sense of purpose, confidence and goodwill. It was perhaps this, above all, that made teaching Teeline to block and day release students such a richly memorable experience.

Chapter 7 Teaching Graduates

SARAH McGHEE

Before the changeover to Teeline at the University of Strathclyde the Postgraduate Diploma in Secretarial Studies had been successfully undertaken by graduates from universities throughout Britain and from overseas. In the early years of the Diploma at the Scottish College of Commerce students had to devote the greater part of their time to shorthand and typewriting, while at the same time they had to study other subjects in depth. As the course was intensive, the theory of shorthand had to be covered in as short a time as possible in order to move on to building up speed. The theory had to be thoroughly studied to achieve worthwhile results and this placed a heavy learning load on students.

In 1964 the Scottish College of Commerce merged with the Royal College of Technology to become the University of Strathclyde. This led to a shorter teaching year and inevitably resulted in a reduction in the number of hours allocated to the skills. It became increasingly clear that something would have to be done in order to retain the high standards.

The problem was solved by asking students to attend classes for 3 extra weeks before the beginning of the university year. This had to go on for many years, for there was no other solution. Members of the staff, conscious of the strain on these students who were committed to doing their best, continually had to think of how the burden could be lightened, particularly with regard to the study of shorthand.

It was not until 1974 that we were made aware of the successes of Teeline. My colleagues and I were fortunate at that time to have a 1-week familiarization course in the system. Most of us were impressed, some more than others. We looked at Teeline initially in its basic form, although we were aware that some changes were being considered. Plans were already afoot to combine the basic Teeline theory with the advanced. Some of the ideas were passed on to us which we were able to make use of, although we had not yet studied the advanced book. I was very much impressed at this stage.

From that moment our thoughts were directed towards the possibility of the change to Teeline from the traditional systems, for more than one system had at some time been taught in the university. Teeline had potential. It could be learned in a shorter time and it was also a highly adaptable system. Was this what we needed? We had to be absolutely sure. Here we had highly intelligent students who had to be able, at the end of their course, to hold down important and responsible posts. Whatever we did, our standard had to remain high.

By good fortune, that same year I taught Teeline in the evening to a

32

young and enthusiastic 16-year-old. While the students at the university were struggling with the study of the traditional shorthand system being taught at the time, this young girl was happily making her way through James Hill's *Basic Teeline*. By Christmas she could take fairly difficult dictation at 50 and 60 w.p.m. Meantime, students at the university had just completed the theory. In March the 16-year-old successfully passed our examination for five minutes at 70 w.p.m. She had had only 70 hours' tuition. After a further 18 hours she passed with distinction the 80 w.p.m. test of Teeline Education Ltd.

This was the proof we needed to assure us that Teeline could be safely and successfully taught to our postgraduate students. In the first experimental year only one group did Teeline. The same number of hours were given to all groups with the extra 3 weeks still included. The Teeline class was a great success, for not only had they achieved the good results but they had done so with a great deal less toil. They also enjoyed learning Teeline and I am convinced, too, that this was a contributory factor to its success. All in the Teeline class passed the shorthand speed test that year.

The following year two groups did Teeline while the other two groups were doing another system for the first time, and because of the success of the Teeline classes, in the following year all the postgraduate students were studying Teeline. Failures there have been during the years, but, human nature being as it is, there will always be those who cannot perform under pressure of writing at speed – for them, speed tests will always present difficulties no matter what system of shorthand is being taught.

Teeline was achieving better results and with less effort. This was important, too, for not only were we looking for a system that could be studied in a shorter term; we were also striving to lighten the learning load of these students who had to study in depth four more subjects.

Need I mention that the 3 extra weeks were no longer needed? By Christmas the students were able to do their first official speed examination. They were able to make use of their shorthand earlier for taking down letters and so at an earlier stage they were producing some worthwhile work. Some were able, during their Easter vacation of one month, to take on more responsible jobs which had hitherto been beyond their capabilities.

How does one approach teaching Teeline to graduates? In my opinion there is not a great deal of difference from teaching it to any other type of student, although one must remember that these students have perhaps just completed three or four years of study in their academic field, so there may be an initial period of orientation. In the first place it is necessary to let them realize the value of daily practice – for proficiency and eventually for speed of writing. Encourage them to have the correct implement for writing – that is, to have a good pen, whether it be fountain or ballpoint – and that it is advantageous to endeavour to have a light hold of the pen, too. This is essential to fast writing and should be mentioned in the early stages of learning.

I do not forbid the use of a pencil but I try to discourage it for the reason that it may not always have a sharp point, so the Teeline notes would not always be as neat and as clear as one would wish.

In Teeline, where there is a choice of outline, let them choose the one that suits them. There is no harm in saying which you prefer and perhaps why you prefer it, but always leave the final choice to them, provided the resulting outline is a legible outline. Legibility is of prime importance throughout. Stress the significance of showing clearly the difference of size of outline. The neglect of watching size leads to many difficulties in reading back the notes.

There is not a great deal of position writing in Teeline, which is one of its many advantages, but I have found that it is worth while giving careful attention to this point in teaching the theory. Those that are important should be stressed at all times. Even small words like *of*, which is above the line and *you* which is on the line; and again, *of course* above the line and *occurs* on the line – simple little words perhaps, but written in the correct position remove the danger of misreading or hesitation in reading.

However, in dealing with them do not take them out of context. They can be emphasized whenever they occur in context to drive home the importance of being precise in this respect. The natural position for writing is on the line and this is the case with most Teeline outlines. So it is worth while watching those that are not on the line.

Whenever there is a misreading, even momentarily, it is helpful to refer to the word misread. Why was it misread? Why was there hesitation? Was the size not shown clearly? Was the outline written carelessly or was it just carelessness in reading? It is worth investigating. All the students present may benefit from the point being dealt with. It is my experience that in many cases all can benefit from a little bit of advice which may have only been required to be directed at one person. This applies to both the reading back and writing/typing back of dictation. Something wrongly transcribed requires to be checked immediately.

In some cases I have found the dictation has been taken down perfectly but wrongly transcribed. If the teacher does not attend to matters like these, which would let students know that they are capable of taking the dictation, and taking it accurately, the students may lose confidence in their ability to use the system. More often than not they may not have taken the time to check such errors when work is returned and the training to do so would be worth while. They become more aware of the fact that carelessness can lead to failure and so the constant reminders lead to good, careful and accurate transcriptions.

It is disconcerting for students, particularly mature students, to see lines and lines of corrections throughout the notes, so avoid this. They become apprehensive when taking dictation and this leads to hesitation in writing, for they will always feel that only the 'correct' outline must go down on paper. Perhaps they have been made aware of the versatility of the system so they are then bewildered when they see so many corrections.

In the early days of dictation, some guidance is needed. The notes should be read through by the teacher and at the end of the passage a few suggestions could be made. This may be in relation to grouping of words or perhaps contracting a common word. If this guidance is given early enough, then the fault is remedied before it gets a firm hold.

Never do anything to stifle their enthusiasm. Show your own enthusiasm for the system all the time. Always encourage the student – even postgraduate students need to be encouraged. They become aware, too, that you are showing some appreciation and are interested in them individually.

Do not insist on always putting down a perfect outline. Generally I advise them to put something down and move on in order to avoid pauses along the way. The outline may not be a good one but it is better than none at all, and for the future use of the word the student may be ready with a better outline.

The blends are used in a large percentage of the writing and if the blended strokes are exaggerated, then the other strokes will take care of themselves. Often students become careless about size and if not remedied early there is difficulty in reading when at some time they discover that their blended strokes are no longer differentiated. A constant reminder will avoid this. Care should also be taken over the small outlines, and those in between take care of themselves.

Should anything be done about the size of writing generally? First and more importantly the outlines should be in proportion. This is essential for easy reading back and avoids the problems of writing strokes of similar size when not intended. Examples of faults that I have found are writing W instead of the WR blend and vice versa; writing *you* so large that it is the same size as *me*. Deal with these points as they occur. They are important and if dealt with in the early stages avoid problems later.

Many people are of the opinion that size does not really matter. There is no doubt in my mind that it takes longer to write bigger outlines. Perhaps it is not advisable nor is it wise to insist that any one writer should cut down the size of writing but in my opinion it is better to let students know that the size could be reduced to advantage. It leads to a neater note-taking, but if it is at the expense of speed then leave it alone.

Each year I have kept some samples of the Teeline written by my students along with their handwritten transcription, and this has encouraged the learners who tended to have careless outlines to endeavour to improve their note-taking. Handwriting in many cases certainly has a bearing on the eventual size and style of outlines written. One of my students who was a very untidy handwriter, after having been encouraged to write Teeline at a reasonable size for several months, noted that her handwriting size and style had improved considerably. This shows that with some encouragement style can be improved and the effort is worth while.

Lay down hard and fast rules about the writing of the outlines and you are spoiling the versatility of the Teeline. I always try to let the students make the final decision.

My experience in teaching Teeline has been confined to the one-year postgraduate course at the university and the highest speed achieved has been 120 w.p.m. for a seven-minute speed test – that is, two passages, one of four minutes' and one of three minutes' duration.

I cover the teaching of theory in 5–6 weeks (8 hours per week) although a fewer number of hours would suffice, but during that time provision is made for the students to do some transcription of their own notes dictated at varying rates. They write their transcriptions until they have become familiar with typewriting and then they type them. It would be inadvisable to present them with two problems at one time – typing from shorthand notes when perhaps they are still not confident with typewriting. I believe that these early 'unseen' dictations are a great preparation for their future production work, which is carried out weekly when theory has been completed.

Try to give them something new to learn every day but always allow time for practising the work previously taught. Never allow them to become bored. Vary the approach from time to time. Give them work to prepare in the evening so that they can start the lesson the following day with familiar work. This allows them to have the thrill of writing faster, particularly when they have prepared the work well. Those who neglect to do so can generally see how the others are progressing and this may encourage them to do something about their own preparation in the future. In the end, all the students of the class are working to capacity.

On occasions in the early stages it may be worth while to ask the students to write a passage leaving one or two lines blank and using these lines to copy at higher rates of speed. This gives them confidence to write faster. This should be done only in the early stages of learning. To continue with this later, when writing has become spontaneous, would only be a hindrance to fast writing.

Changing to Teeline presented opportunities for new developments in other spheres, for example, in word processing. It has enabled the department to devote more time to other activities in the field of new technology. This is what is required today – a system of shorthand that can be learned quickly and efficiently. Those who have taught other systems of shorthand, as I have myself, have nothing to fear in changing to Teeline. It has a great deal to offer.

The results I have achieved since teaching Teeline have been much better, and all achieved in a considerably shorter time and with much less energy expended. Enthusiasm for the system is essential and this is where you, the teacher, can play your part. You have to show that the system works. You have to guide the students, no matter what their ability, whether they be university graduates or just 16-year-olds at school. The inventor of the system said 'If you can write, you can write Teeline'. Should there be any difficulties? I do not think so. This system knows no bounds.

Editor's note: Teeline is also taught on the following degree courses:

The Dip. HE/BA in Languages for Business course at the Polytechnic, Wolverhampton. This was the first secretarial-linguist course in the country to gain validation as a national award, and was approved by the Council for National Academic Awards in 1981.

The BA in Secretarial Skills at Humberside College of Higher Education, both full-time and part-time courses. The teaching of Teeline on both courses begun in September 1984.

Chapter 8 Teeline on TOPS Courses

JUNE HASKELL

Courses under the Training Opportunities Scheme (TOPS) have been held at Spelthorne Adult Education Institute, Staines, for fifteen years. As an adult education institute it has never had the benefits of facilities, resources and available money that other educational establishments have enjoyed, yet despite apparent inadequacies, the TOPS courses have been successful. Students leave, after training, with renewed confidence and with prospects of good employment.

Two courses are offered: audio-typewriting/shorthand and secretarial skills.

The audio students attend for 18 weeks and study communication and office practice (which are internally examined), typewriting to RSA Stage II, audio-typewriting to Stage II and Teeline. They are also offered 2 weeks of work experience with local firms.

The secretarial students attend for 31 weeks and also have 2 weeks' work experience. The subjects studied are: structure of business, secretarial procedures, communication, typewriting, audio-typewriting and Teeline.

Some single subject examinations are taken throughout the year, but the aim of the course is to enter students for the London Chamber of Commerce and Industry Private Secretary's Certificate in June. Some students from either course may wish to enter for RSA Typewriting Stage III, about half of whom will pass and a small number will gain distinctions. The Training Services Department (TSD) pay for most of the examinations.

Prospective students apply to their local job centre or employment office and are vetted for suitability. They then attend an appropriate college or adult institute for further interviews by a representative of the Training Services Department of the Manpower Services Commission and a college lecturer (or lecturers) with special responsibility for TOPS.

The applicants are required to have a minimum entry qualification of O level English but sometimes more mature applicants would not have taken this examination and, provided they appear suitable, they will be asked to take a simple English test. This test contains sentences where missing words have to be chosen from those given in brackets – for instance, a choice of *its/it's*, *lose/loose*, *there/their*, etc. Another section necessitates the insertion of apostrophes in the right places; yet another, the identification of wrongly spelt words in a passage and the correct spellings substituted. In addition, all applicants have to write eight

commonly misspelt words such as *occurred* and *separate*. This gives a
good assessment of the applicant's usage of English.

Those who come for interview with a fixed idea of the course they
would like to pursue may, on close questioning, be found more suitable
for the alternative course, or even be recommended to take one in
another institute. It is essential to accept students who have the right
motivation to attend regularly and punctually, apply themselves to the
work, achieve good results in the examinations and, most of all, obtain
worthwhile full-time employment at the end of the course.

There is a 3-week probationary period at the beginning of the courses
for adjustments to be made on both sides. If the college decides that a
course is unsuitable for a student then they may be asked to leave, but
this would leave them eligible to apply for another course later on. If
students feel they are not able to cope with the work or their
private commitments will not allow them to continue, then the same
rule applies. Only rarely will the student be able to change from one
course to another, because the alternative class will already be full.

Students receive a training allowance while on a course, which is paid
weekly by Giro cheque. Besides the basic allowance, which is tax free and
includes free credits of National Insurance contributions, they will also
receive a travel allowance, if necessary, and a small sum to cover the cost
of a midday meal. They may also be entitled to an earnings-related
supplement if they have left a job in order to start training. All this adds
up to a considerable sum, and most students are well aware of the
benefits they are receiving and will show their appreciation by attending
lessons regularly and punctually.

However, as is human nature, one or two people may regard TOPS as
an easy option; close watch will be kept and reports concerning them
will be sent to the TSD who will finally ask them to terminate the
course if all warnings have failed to alter their conduct. This will
preclude them from joining another course. The TSD also visit the
classes at intervals both to monitor their progress and to hear their
grumbles and criticisms, if any.

Students and their problems

Students on TOPS courses have to be at least 19 years old and away
from full-time education for two years before they are accepted. The
range of ages is considerable, perhaps from 19 to 55. The majority, as
may be expected, are women, although one or two men have been
welcomed into the classes. There is usually little integration between
students of different courses. This may be more a result of lesson
arrangements which give students their breaks at varying times, rather
than their separate aims and objectives.

Students will have been engaged in a variety of work before they apply for a TOPS course. They may have been nurses, hairdressers, school dinner ladies, teachers, airline stewardesses, or have spent several years in raising families. Their reasons for becoming students again will be just as varied, ranging from the need to update their skills, from their dissatisfaction in previous jobs, from their hesitation in seeking employment because of lack of training, or from redundancy. One lady had never been engaged in paid employment at all, having gone straight from school into marriage and brought up a family before bravely seeking training and employment. In a few months she had achieved both.

However stringent the vetting might have been at the beginning, hitherto undisclosed problems may arise once the course begins. Illnesses such as migraines, back trouble, or even epilepsy, may prevent some students from giving of their best in lessons. Marital or family problems may cause worry and distress. Bereavements occur. Students may not have realized they were short-sighted or a little hard of hearing until they had to read from the board or listen to audio tapes. Counselling and advice must always be available, while sometimes a friendly ear will be enough to enable students to sort out their own troubles.

Course comparisons

Teeline was introduced at the Spelthorne Institute in 1971 and is now used exclusively for TOPS courses because of its short learning time and its good results. It is popular with students, who say it is a logical system. Fair trial was given to another system on the secretarial course but, when two parallel courses were run, it was obvious which of the two systems was the more suitable for these comparatively short courses. It was not only that Teeline produced better results, but it was clearly observed that the system of shorthand used affected all other subjects. Those studying Teeline were noticeably more at ease in their other classes, while the other students had to work far harder at their shorthand, and the pressure remained with them through the whole of the course. On the 18-week sessions, it would not have been possible to teach any other system to proficiency in the allotted weekly total of 9 hours' lesson time. With Teeline, speeds up to 90 w.p.m. have regularly been attained on the 18-week courses and up to 110–120 w.p.m. on the secretarial course.

The Manpower Services Commission finds Teeline a cost-effective system because of the short learning period and the accuracy of transcription. The London Chamber of Commerce and Industry finds that Teeline writers do very well in their shorthand examinations and that 'most shorthand examination distinctions and credits are gained by writers of the Teeline method'.

It has been found advisable to introduce the main parts of Teeline theory in as short a time as possible, certainly no longer than 3 weeks (or

27 hours) on these courses. When easy dictation is given and further, more advanced, outlines become possible, these can be touched on quickly at the time they occur. Later on, when these can be explored more fully, the students have already had some advance warning of ways of reducing outlines or facilitating the writing of them.

Constant revision is necessary but need not always be deliberately planned. The students themselves will raise questions about particular outlines, and these will act as reminders to the rest of the class. Ideas are always welcome from the students – this is, indeed, how Teeline has grown into its present form. Alternative outlines on the board will allow the students to practise those which they find easiest to write and to read back. They are encouraged to keep to the rules and not to deviate too far from what are, after all, well-proven outlines as shown in the textbooks.

It has been noticed that those people who insist on writing an 's' inside an angle and outside a curve, contrary to what is recommended, are the ones who do not reach high speeds, and who find most difficulty in reading their outlines.

Regular transcription tests are given. These show up weaknesses in spelling and punctuation that can be remedied both in the shorthand and communication classes.

It is a great help if teachers can talk over the difficulties they encounter and tackle them together. After all, they are endeavouring to create a secretary and there must be a transfer of learning from one subject to all the others. This is also why, at every possible opportunity, transcription should be done on a typewriter. It makes no sense to write transcriptions by hand, since this will seldom be called for in a work situation. When typewriters are not available, a word with the typewriting teacher may enable students to type from their notes in the warming-up part of the lesson. Examination authorities indicate a move towards all shorthand transcriptions being typewritten in examinations.

Speed tests should also be given at regular intervals. They show the students how they are progressing. They also reveal the vast range of ability or concentration in a class. But speed cannot be attained without proper grounding in theory. Drills are not often given in class, but there may be plenty of pauses in lessons when practice of outlines is possible.

To help in instant recognition, flash cards are used that show contracted outlines and special forms. Small cards that have common word outlines written on them may be shuffled to produce different combinations and read at increasing speeds. Students can be given turns at reading them too.

Teachers record dictation cassettes for use in their classes. By sharing these with each other, they can offer different voices to work from. Students often like to use these at home but it has been found that lending so often means losing, so students have been encouraged to buy cheap C60 cassettes and copies of the tapes are made for them on a tape-copier.

Tapes can also be used in class to vary the lessons but students prefer 'live' dictation if the teacher is there. However, it has been found very useful to use the cassette recorders in the language laboratory. These are in booths with headphones and it means that the teacher can work with slower students while faster ones are using the cassettes, or vice versa. Recordings can also be made on cassette while the teacher is dictating and can be played back both to give the students more practice on the piece and to verify what the teacher has said!

Students must be pressed to indicate the ends of sentences, since the sense of a passage can so easily be changed by substituting the end of one sentence for the beginning of another.

Dictation is given as recommended in all books on shorthand – a variety of easy and difficult material, long pieces for stamina and short pieces for sprints and various speeds to suit everyone. Plenty of reading is required, both from the class as a whole or with each person reading one sentence aloud. Pieces are sometimes given as a hand-out for students to prepare overnight ready for dictation next day. Apart from these, and their personal commitment with tapes, hardly any homework is set. On these courses there is a good deal of written work to be completed for communication and office practice, for instance, and it is not considered necessary to overload the students with extra tasks when most of them have homes to run and families to look after, and when Teeline results at the end of the course are already so satisfactory.

Although every effort is made to offer a variety of dictation passages taken from all types of shorthand books and magazines we cannot prepare students for all eventualities in their future employment, but there is no reason why they should not compile a glossary of the particular terms they need in their jobs. They can then use Teeline in whichever line of business they find themselves.

To vary lessons, students can write passages on the board, can take turns at dictation, change over notebooks for reading, take very slow dictation for immaculate outlines, and always crib as much as possible from their neighbours in the hope of finding easier or better outlines. They can write a sentence of, say, twelve to fourteen words on one line and then see how many times they can repeat the line in 30 seconds. In the last part of Friday afternoon a crossword or word game can be introduced. 'How many words can you make from the word "shorthand"? Write them in Teeline as well.' Above all, teachers should show their enthusiasm and liking for the system and keep their students looking forward to the next lesson.

When examinations are imminent, adequate preparation is given by the use of actual examination matter and at least one mock exam. *Teeline Shorthand Dictation Passages* is especially useful in this respect. It has been possible to arrange the first Teeline examination for the eighth week of the course, particularly for the 18-week students, who otherwise might have to wait till the end of the course before taking their first examination. Most students will achieve 50 w.p.m. by this time, and several will succeed at 60. At the end of 18 weeks, both groups will enter for examinations, the aim being at least 80 or even 90 w.p.m.

Teeline has allowed TOPS to offer a system of shorthand on short courses which can be developed to speeds not only adequate for employment, but capable of further development to whatever speed is required.

Chapter 9 Teaching Medical Secretaries

NANCY BLAIR

Anniesland College, Glasgow, has been running a two-year medical secretarial course since 1965. At first the shorthand lessons were given in another system, and I was responsible for the change to Teeline in 1973. A number of my colleagues were somewhat apprehensive at what at first seemed a revolutionary change, but they soon became wholehearted in their support.

Since the decision to adopt Teeline was made, Anniesland College has built a good reputation with a success rate of around 85 per cent over the years.

The RSA Medical Shorthand-Typists' Certificate and the RSA 100 w.p.m. medical shorthand examinations are two of the compulsory certificates towards gaining the Medical Secretarial Diploma. Students must also obtain passes in four other subjects: medical secretarial practice and office procedures; English; social services; and medical terminology and clinical procedures; therefore the more quickly the shorthand and typing sections are completed, the better.

When the change was first made, two classes ran in parallel so that results could be compared. These classes were not streamed in any way but simply divided alphabetically, according to their surnames. At the end of the course, the Teeline class had a pass rate of 84 per cent compared with 54 per cent in the other system. About one-third of the Teeline class also obtained certificates for 120 w.p.m. in medical stenography.

Since then, all medical secretarial students have been taught Teeline and results have been consistently good. Two students from Anniesland have passed at 140 w.p.m.

It has been found that Teeline medical shorthand has been more enjoyable and satisfying for the students and for the lecturers. Even for the occasional student who finds skill subjects difficult, Teeline is an easier hurdle because of the shorter time taken to cover the theory, which leaves more time, energy and concentration for other subjects. Shorthand has become a popular subject since the advent of Teeline.

At Anniesland College, students go on field-work to a health centre for 2 weeks in the first year of the course and in the second year they spend 6 weeks in hospitals and in general medical practices. As the theory of Teeline can be covered within a few weeks from the beginning of training, students are soon able to use it for note-taking. This is a valuable asset on field-work, where a variety of duties are undertaken, and they find it is a skill greatly appreciated by doctors and administrators.

Students are introduced to medical Teeline towards the end of their first year, after they have obtained a 90 or 100 w.p.m. certificate in non-specialized shorthand. This is because it is considered wiser not to introduce any specialized vocabulary before reaching that degree of proficiency in everyday language.

At the outset students are a little overwhelmed by the idea of writing in shorthand such words as *nephrectomy, osteomyelitis, chondromalacia,* etc., but as so many medical words can be broken up into roots, prefixes and suffixes, and special abbreviations can be used (particularly in the two latter categories), they quickly accept and enjoy the challenge.

Their quick adaptability to medical shorthand is helped by the fact that during their first year they have been learning medical terminology, meanings of words, spelling, pronunciation, and receiving instruction in anatomy and physiology, first aid and clinical procedures, etc.

The majority of Anniesland students leave college with 100 w.p.m. in medical shorthand. The few who do not, have at least gained a pass in the Medical Shorthand-Typists' Certificate. On average, about one-third to one-quarter of the students reach 120 w.p.m. in medical Teeline. In some parts of the country medical secretaries receive extra allowances if they gain the higher certificates.

Job prospects are good, with openings in general medical practices, health centres and large group practices where promotion to the position of practice administrator is possible. There are also posts in medical research establishments, medical insurance companies and pharmaceutical firms.

However, hospitals are the biggest employers of medical secretaries and a wide variety of extremely interesting jobs may be obtained. One of the most satisfying positions is that of unit secretary – that is, working with a hospital consultant and his/her team. Being an integral and necessary part of this team gives the medical secretary an important role to play in the efficient and smooth running of the administrative procedures so 'necessary for the overall care of patients. Some consultants insist on having their secretaries accompany them on their ward rounds, so that they can dictate notes on patients immediately after examining them.

The objectives of the Anniesland College course are:

First year (average of 7–8 hours per week over 38 weeks, starting in mid-August): November, RSA 50/60 w.p.m., or December SCOTBEC 60/70/80. March, RSA 80 w.p.m. June, SCOTBEC 90/100 w.p.m. Some medical material is introduced during the last 2 weeks of the first year.
Second year (average of 7–8 hours over 34 weeks (extra field-work) starting mid-August): November, RSA Medical Shorthand-Typists'

Certificate Stage II. March, RSA 100 w.p.m. medical stenography. June, SCOTBEC 100/120/140 w.p.m. medical stenography.

Having taught shorthand to medical secretaries in two different systems from 1965 to the present, I am in an excellent position to be able to dwell favourably on the advantages of Teeline. There is no doubt in my mind that in learning the system, these students have a great lead over those who do not, in that they achieve more in less time, and they do it with a great feeling of success and satisfaction.

Chapter 10 The Bilingual Secretary

I French Teeline   ANN HARVEY

We first heard of Teeline at Oxford College of Further Education when the lecturer in charge of shorthand and typewriting acted as marker for one of the shorthand examining bodies during an Easter break. He noticed the good results, looked at the notes to see which system was used and discovered Teeline.

During the summer vacation, staff were asked to learn Teeline. On our return, we soon found the system was acceptable to students because there was much less theory to learn, much less memory load, and there was moderate speed coming right from the start.

We had two problems at college. We had been running a bilingual secretarial course for some years, offering either French or German as a main language. The system then in use adapted well to French and we were getting good results by the end of the two-year course; but – and this was the first problem – in German the system was cumbersome. The other was that we had a group of bilingual students from the local polytechnic who came only four mornings a week, so this was really a crash course.

Teeline proved to be the answer to both difficulties. It adapts easily to German as well as French and has a much shorter learning time.

My plans for adapting Teeline to French involved meeting the discoverer of Teeline, James Hill. He thought the idea would work and we spent some hours discussing it. The system evolved gradually and I incorporated many ideas from students with my own. There is always someone in a class who has a gift for seeing a neat outline, and we learned from experience.

For instance, 'q' is a letter frequently used in French, with *que, qui, quoi, quand*, etc. Some of the students found they were misreading their 'q' for a badly written PR, so James Hill suggested a different derivation of the handwritten 'qu' which we adopted.

Otherwise, we follow the English Teeline theory very closely and students apply all they learn in English to their French. So many words are spelt the same, or nearly the same, that the outlines are there for us and in this way students reinforce their learning. Without realizing it, they revise their blends and abbreviations.

We have had to make special provision for features that are peculiar to the French language – the mute endings, or endings that sound the same but which must be worked out correctly at transcription stage (e.g. *acheter, acheté, achetez* – and even *achetait* sounds only marginally different). Further, the student must be able to understand the text as it is read if confusion is to be avoided between similar-sounding phrases, such as *vous en auriez* and *vous honoriez*.

At first I thought we would need more vowels in French notes than in English, but this is not so. Once students become experienced, they read their notes back amazingly well and are able to resort to the dictionary for help in transcribing the outline for an unfamiliar term.

French Teeline greatly extends students' working knowledge of business French and, above all, demands that they are accurate with their grammar. Eventually it becomes automatic to make the correct agreements as they type their transcriptions.

Moreover, I can incorporate in dictation sessions material that is useful for their language examinations. When such material has been dictated, read back, and perhaps repeated at a higher speed, it is likely to stick in the mind and therefore can be recalled when they compose essays and letters.

Over the years I have altered the teaching text to make it more commercial and business orientated. A French colleague has recorded the text on cassettes at increasing speeds and this makes it virtually a self-tuition course. Past examination papers are obtainable from the London Chamber of Commerce and Industry and the Royal Society of Arts, so there is no shortage of dictation material.

It is important that students have a good standard of French before they tackle French shorthand in any system. Learning shorthand in a second language is a complex process, requiring the combination of three skills – to hear spoken French, take it down in shorthand, and then produce an accurate typewritten transcript. It is essential that they have a good understanding of grammar and my personal view is that anyone without A level French should not be expected to do it.

Like most teachers in my department, I had initial doubts about Teeline but it was soon found that we could get good results with (and this is the vital point) a much shorter learning time.

We start French Teeline at the beginning of the course (students are post-A level standard, aged 18 or 19 years) with a daily lesson of 45 minutes. They reach speeds of 60–80 w.p.m. at the end of the first year (36 weeks) and speeds of 90–120 at the end of the second year. In addition, students have 5 hours of English Teeline and 7 hours of typewriting a week, as well as 8 hours a week on the various aspects of work in their second language.

Recent results in the French shorthand examinations of London Chamber of Commerce and Industry show that of nine students specializing in French, all passed at 90 w.p.m. in May of their second year; six of them also passed at 100 (four with distinction). Five of them attempted the 120 w.p.m. test and, of these, three passed with distinction and two failed. Some years one or two of our students are placed 'first in the United Kingdom' at different speeds and once an outstanding student achieved this honour at 110 w.p.m. These results, and similar ones from earlier years, show that French Teeline can stand its ground.

I said earlier that Teeline has a much shorter learning time. With the hours that have been saved we have been able to incorporate a subsidiary language in the linguists' course during the second year. This is a tremendous asset to students for not only are they able to offer their main language to a high degree of proficiency, but also Spanish or Italian. This allows them to use their subsidiary language for dealing with phone calls, to understand a letter coming into an office, and perhaps to draw up a comprehensive reply. All this makes a secretary far more useful.

With the increasing use of word processors, will shorthand die out as a secretarial skill? I think not, in the foreseeable future, at this level of bilingual work.

II German Teeline FRANCES J. BURTON and ULRIKE PARKINSON

Teeline adapts to German much more easily than the shorthand system previously used at Oxford College of Further Education. The fewer hours required for students to master Teeline allows time for a subsidiary language to be added to the curriculum.

It is often assumed that students actually learn the German shorthand system known as the *Einheitssystem*, a system that was created in 1924 from the numerous shorthand systems which had emerged in Germany in the nineteenth century. It has a basic form and a high speed form, uses thick and thin strokes and three sizes of outline. Although it is a complicated system to learn, verbatim writers in the Bundestag can achieve 500 syllables a minute. Schoolchildren often start to learn privately at an early age.

There would be no point in students attempting to learn two different systems when the Teeline system they learn in their mother tongue adapts so well. A great asset of Teeline is that if students miss a few lessons through illness, they do not fall irrevocably behind without hope of catching up. Some students feel so confident that they voluntarily undertake the study of an additional foreign language adaptation, and often take examinations in two foreign languages.

German Teeline is taught to three categories of student: graduates and Oxford Polytechnic students in the final year of a three-year language course, who each do a one-year secretarial training, and post-A level students who do a two-year course.

Because there are fewer students offering German, it is sometimes necessary to combine the students into one group for German Teeline, thus creating a mixed-ability class. The fact that they are encountering business German for the first time levels things out somewhat and often the graduate students are kind, helpful and supportive to the younger ones.

All students train for the LCCI and RSA German shorthand examinations, and the aim is to provide them with a valuable skill for use in jobs at home and abroad.

The immediate requirement of students is to acquire a knowledge of commerce. Obviously a bilingual secretarial course will include a substantial number of hours' tuition in the language which will include revision of grammar and structures, commercial and economic background and business communications. German Teeline classes can reinforce the new vocabulary but specific instruction in such terms as *letter of credit, bill of lading, bill of exchange*, etc. is essential. Without office experience, and not being directly involved, students have difficulty in knowing who is who in a business communication and hence have difficulty with pronouns. In addition, special attention is paid to the up-to-date vocabulary found in the advertisements for word processors and the like – terms that have not yet filtered through to reference books and dictionaries.

Teaching material in class not only serves the purpose of teaching German Teeline, but serves the much wider aims and objectives of enlarging German commercial vocabulary. It is gratifying and encouraging for students to find that vocabulary covered in a language lesson crops up again in the Teeline lesson. The German Teeline teacher is constantly on the look-out for new and relevant material in newspapers and magazines, and this helps to make lessons interesting and varied.

Ideally, students should have a good basic knowledge of the language, and a wide passive – if not active – vocabulary. Those who have spent a considerable time in a German-speaking country, or who have a German parent, naturally comprehend better but this is no compensation for poor written German.

It is also important that students improve their general knowledge by reading English newspapers and periodicals and by taking an interest in current affairs. This can be integrated with a business affairs or commerce class covering such topical things as inflation and balance of payments.

Students tend to succeed with German Teeline in proportion to their grasp of German grammar, their ability to comprehend the vocabulary and complicated structures, as well as their aptitude for shorthand in general.

German Teeline is usually started 2–4 weeks after students have been introduced to the English Teeline system. In this way the lessons serve as reinforcement and consolidation. There is no reason why the German adaptation should not be introduced immediately, provided the students' knowledge of the language is really good.

As a rule, students receive four lessons per week, totalling about $3\frac{1}{2}$ hours. This is sufficient to enable more mature and able students to reach up to 120 syllables per minute (s.p.m.) and the A-level people to reach 90–105 s.p.m. by the middle of May when the LCCI German shorthand examinations are held. This means that while the College of Further Education students have had approximately 30 weeks' tuition, the Polytechnic students, with a shorter year, have received about 26 weeks' tuition.

As the new curricula envisage fewer hours spent on acquiring skills such as shorthand, $3\frac{1}{2}$ hours per week may be regarded as too much. Anything less, though, would have to be regarded as merely providing students with an introduction to the subject. To give students real competence based on experience, 45 minutes per working day would be ideal.

It is important that students understand the text. Teachers should anticipate difficulties, translate words and explain structures. In particular, in a business letter where the sender is writing to the addressee about a third or even a fourth party, the sense can become very confusing for the student and it helps if the background is explained. They should be encouraged to carry a pocket dictionary at all times. Constant checking is required to ensure that they are acquiring the new vocabulary.

German Teeline is adapted from the English system and although the frequency of occurrence of certain prefixes and suffixes makes a slightly different order desirable, the same rules apply. It has been found that giving the Teeline characters together with the text makes the learning process much easier for the student. Remember that they may find a word completely new; therefore the Teeline character, without help, becomes indecipherable, thus creating the idea that it is difficult to master.

Practise the alphabet, pointing out the differences from the English. Dictate the text slowly while students copy from the book, leaving blank lines for repeats. Read back from own notes. Constantly check that the words and text are understood, for students are sometimes reluctant to ask. Classwork can be slow, and therefore some preparation by students is desirable. Once started, they can prepare the text for homework, leaving blank lines.

Each lesson should contain continuous revision of the system from the beginning, as well as revision of the vocabulary. As students gain confidence class activity can be varied by:

1. dictating new material, first demonstrating new words, abbreviations and word groupings;

2. preparing practice passages in Teeline with a clear space between lines for filling in from slow dictation;

3. typing out German text with blank lines for insertion of characters by students for homework. Characters can then be checked for accuracy;

4. writing some new Teeline on the blackboard for students to read, then dictating it;

5. asking each student to translate a typical business sentence into English and subsequently putting it back into German.

There is no point in trying to create connected outlines for all compound words. The individual components may occur over and over again, while the compound form occurs only rarely. Each part, however, should be written close together.

Keep dictation short. One minute, rising to two, is long enough. As concentration skills cannot be assumed at this stage, they must also be trained. Sometimes students tend to concentrate so hard on the Teeline characters that quite often (unless their German is really first class), they cannot take in the sense of a passage. Therefore, brevity with a variety of material containing oft-repeated words, creates an understanding of common phrases and business sentences.

The students are sometimes disconcerted when first encountering commercial language. They are accustomed to feeling that their German is good, and to come across a whole area of language that initially is virtually incomprehensible can be daunting for them. Give them every assistance so that confidence is built rather than destroyed.

When progress through the textbook has reached the suffix -ANK, extra text can be introduced and used for dictation practice.

No effort is made to get to the end of the textbook in a certain time or before introducing supplementary text. The prefixes and suffixes towards the end of the textbook occur sufficiently infrequently for them to be demonstrated in advance on a need-to-know basis if necessary. Progress through the book can gradually slow down, allowing more time for revision and new text of more interest to the students.

German Teeline tapes are an important feature in speed-building. They can be used for homework as many students nowadays possess cassette recorders, or in the language laboratory in free periods. Tapes can cater for individual needs and many students like to practise at home and in vacations.

Tapes can be used as learning aids either on their own or as part of learning packages. With more students opting for distance learning, this method of teaching will come into its own, but even for students attending a regular course, a learning package can be used successfully. The teacher can prepare the printed material in advance and record tapes to reinforce the theory covered and hand out these packages to students to work through at their own pace without the pressure inherent in class.

This method not only helps the teacher in that a lot of theory can be taught quickly; it is also welcomed by students, as they appreciate the variety of method and the fact that they can work at their own individual pace in small guided steps. This is particularly beneficial for weaker students as it gives them a feeling of achievement when working independently and monitoring their own progress.

Computers do not yet play a part in the learning of shorthand, but if a college has one at its disposal, the teaching of commercial vocabulary could be reinforced by computer-assisted learning.

If students have already started English Teeline, they will have received tuition and guidance in writing the characters. Some think the characters are written along the line like handwriting and they have difficulty in understanding how blends are made. Demonstrate, and keep an eye on size, accuracy and method of writing, without giving any feeling that there is a right way and a wrong way. The modern tendency of 'anything goes' with handwriting often leads to difficulty because the students are unaccustomed to controlling their hands, or they may hold the pen in an unusual manner.

Accuracy is essential because words such as *um, mit, und, das, des, beste, besondere, weiter, wieder, grössere, grösser, im, immer, jeden, guten, von, vom, am* may easily be misrendered.

In the German textbook the Teeline characters are not always written the same way. Students may point out, for instance, that in some cases *Fabrik* starts on the line, in some cases above it. It does not matter – a rigid approach is not desirable. It does matter, however, that words commencing with a 't' are written in the T position.

In creating the adaptation, certain difficulties arose. The verbs *werden, wurden, würden, worden*, have the same consonants. The only satisfactory way to differentiate them is to use vowel indicators in the character, even if in the wrong place, or outside the character, or as an umlaut marker. Another problem was with *in* and *ein*. Students sometimes have difficulty dissociating *in* in German from *in* in English, but obviously in German a distinction must be made.

In some characters such as *wohl, bestehen, stehen, beziehen*, H, although silent, is retained because it helps to make a flowing outline and, more importantly, renders it easily recognizable. However, H may naturally be omitted if the writer prefers.

The device in English Teeline for substituting C for K, especially when the latter is followed by T or R, may also be applied to German for such words as *der Markt, das Risiko*. It must be left to the discretion of the teacher or writer, however, to decide whether this may be done safely without confusion.

In German Teeline, L can often go either up or down. Where D or T follows L, the downward form is preferred to avoid unnecessary disjoining. On the other hand, to avoid characters with three or more downward strokes, the upward form is sometimes preferred. On occasion, one or the other just makes a better join.

Teeline Z occurs more often in German, but as described in the textbook, S can be substituted to good effect. In the German textbook Z is usually retained at the beginning of words and sometimes in the middle. If students feel it will not confuse them, however, S plus vowel indicator U or E (downward form) could be used instead for such words as *das Ziel, zurückzuführen*, and so on, to create more fluent and streamlined characters.

Nothing is gained by harassing the students, but good habits, such as putting in full stops, lead to much better transcriptions.

When making abbreviations of adjectives it is a good idea to show unequivocally the beginnings and the endings so that there is no room for mistake.

When giving dictation, the teacher should enunciate endings as clearly as possible. Without an excellent knowledge of German grammar, students have difficulty with the endings. Coaching in basic grammar may be necessary during shorthand lessons.

Try to make a clear distinction between -E and -ER endings. For extra clarity, and in line with audio and telephone usage, *zwo* for *zwei*, *Julei* for *Juli* may be dictated.

In Germany, shorthand is counted in syllables. If you have to count out your own material, it becomes quite quick and easy, with practice, to count the syllables which are then best marked every twenty. If, on the other hand, you have material counted in words, the usual conversion is $1\frac{1}{2}$ syllables to the word, i.e. 15 syllables equals 10 words.

As soon as students can cope with unseen dictation at 60 s.p.m. (40 w.p.m.), a weekly handwritten transcription can be given for homework. Encourage students to ask if they have missed something out or not understood a word. They *want* to get it right and their morale is improved if they are given help to achieve it. They learn nothing by transcribing rubbish. Always bear in mind the aim of improving their German. Handwritten transcription prepares students for the LCCI examinations.

The RSA examinations are typewritten and this also requires practice. When competency in typewriting is reaching RSA Stage I standard, introduce German typewriting so that the DIN[1] recommendations for typing can be learnt. At least one weekly typewritten transcription should be allowed for, gradually increasing in speed and length. For this the classroom should be equipped with good dictionaries.

Students will have difficulty with the pronouns *ihr* and *sie*, especially in business letters. Comparatives of adjectives taking an umlaut are often not perfectly understood, nor strong verbs in the third person and past participle. Frequently they do not get the sense of the tense and misrender such words as *sandten*. Plurals and the subjunctive tense can also create difficulties. Common errors are *unserer* for *unser*, confusion over *der Wunsch, dem Wunsche, die Wünsche* and *wünschen, dem Grunde* and *die Gründe, den Gründen, steigen, steigern, legen, liegen, die Lage* and *das Lager.* It is all due to imperfect understanding and lack of comprehension; therefore the more frequently students read and listen to German, the better.

The punctuation of German prose is much more formalized than the punctuation of English. Students need to be aware of the rules and make every effort to apply them.

As always, one is faced with the necessity for training students realistically but at the same time equipping them to pass examinations. Test pieces often contain structures not usually encountered in actual German business communications, e.g. *des Monats, in der Anlage,* yet one is obliged to make the students aware of the possibility of their occurrence.

With practice, students naturally become quite good at business letters or business oriented passages, but those of a more general nature always present a challenge. Teachers will find they may have to dictate these much more slowly, and give more help with them.

Examinations in German shorthand are offered by the LCCI and RSA. The LCCI examination has two stages: elementary (50–60 w.p.m.) and intermediate (70–100 w.p.m.). The examination consists of one four-minute passage of a commercial nature with handwritten transcription. The RSA examinations are at 80, 100 and 120 s.p.m. and consist of two three-minute passages with typewritten transcription. The examination at 140 s.p.m. has been discontinued. Dictionaries are allowed in both examinations. Further details may be obtained from the relevant examining bodies.

What can realistically be achieved? After one year, A level students are usually capable of LCCI 70 w.p.m. and/or RSA 80/100 s.p.m.; graduates up to LCCI 80/90 w.p.m. and RSA 120 s.p.m. After two years the A level candidates can usually achieve the top speeds in both examinations. The occasional graduate who does two years can easily attain the top speeds.

The LCCI intermediate examination has a wide spread of speeds, therefore students usually have two attempts in order to make sure of a lower speed and to attempt a higher one.

When entering candidates, it must be borne in mind that the LCCI examinations are usually held in the middle of May, and the RSA in the middle of June, after the Spring bank holiday. Over the years numerous prizes in German Teeline have been awarded to students at Oxford College of Further Education, the highest being for LCCI 80 w.p.m. At the highest speeds the number of candidates in the entire country is a mere handful. Good speeds can comfortably be achieved, but the candidate must have sufficiently good German to make an accurate transcription.

All this makes bilingual secretaries offering German as their main language something of a rarity. Up to the present, students have been able to get jobs in Germany quite easily. Ex-students have worked, or are working, for the Student *Austauschdienst* in Bonn, Rowenta and the Mellon Bank in Frankfurt, shipping agents in Hamburg, Reuters and Austrian Radio in Vienna.

Students acquire jobs in a variety of ways – from advertisements, by writing letters of enquiry to firms, and from offers received from previous employers. There are, of course, always jobs available in London and they occur in the provinces as well. Employers are usually very impressed by the standard that students have achieved in German Teeline; in Germany 140 s.p.m. is considered to be a good speed.

A most important factor in teaching German Teeline is getting hold of suitable material, not only for dictation but also to encourage the students to improve their language. In this connection the following publications are very useful:

Frances J. Burton and Germa Meder, *German Teeline*. Available from Teeline Education Ltd, Haywood, Queen Street, Helensburgh, Dunbartonshire G84 9QQ.

Winklers Illustrierte, a monthly magazine for stenographers containing dictation material. Winklers Verlag, Gebrüder Grimm, 6100 Darmstadt.

Musterdiktate für Kurzschrift, Maschinenschreiben und Phonotypie, a monthly magazine for stenographers containing dictation material. Heckners Verlag, Postfach 260, 3340 Wolfenbüttel.

Unsere Zeitung, a student newspaper containing a digest of articles from the German press with *Lesehilfe*. Published monthly. Bookpostgiro, 39 Church Road, Watford WD1 3PY.

Scala
Jugendmagazin, published bi-monthly and available free of charge for educational groups;
Monatszeitschrift, published monthly and available on subscription, but more suitable for older students.
Scala International, Frankfurter Societäts-Druckerei GmbH, Postfach 29 29, Frankenallee 71–81, 6000 Frankfurt am Main 1.

Frances J. Burton and Germa Meder, *Die deutsche Sekretärin* (Cassell). Gives DIN rules for typewriting and audio, with exercises for RSA examinations.

German dictation tapes are available from Ulrike Parkinson, Oxford College of Further Education, Oxpens Road, Oxford OX1 1SA.

---

[1] *Editor's note:* the DIN recommendations refer to *Deutsche Industrie Norm*, the standardization recommendations of the *Deutsches Institut für Normung*, which is the equivalent of the British Standards Institution.

III Spanish Teeline   JOAN McCLUNG and ROBERT ORR

As Teeline is based on the alphabet, it follows that many foreign languages which share the same letters as English may be adapted into the system, but obviously a good knowledge of a foreign language is essential before embarking on a Teeline adaptation.

In the light of our experience at Belfast College of Business Studies, we have found that a good A level student on a two-year bilingual course can produce quite remarkable results with Teeline. They usually achieve 120–140 w.p.m. in the RSA shorthand examination and 90–100 w.p.m. in two foreign languages in RSA and LCCI tests. The one-year postgraduate intensive course can produce results of 100 w.p.m. in English Teeline and 80 + in one foreign language.

The allocation of time to shorthand for post-A level groups (a two-year course) is $4\frac{1}{2}$ hours a week in English Teeline, 2 hours a week in French Teeline and 2 hours a week in Spanish or German Teeline. On the postgraduate one-year intensive course, there are 5 hours a week in English Teeline and 2 hours a week in their second language Teeline (either Spanish, French or German).

The timing of the presentation of language Teeline is important. It is felt better to wait until 2 or 3 weeks have elapsed before presenting classes with foreign language Teeline. This gives students time to become accustomed to the idea of doing English Teeline first and then the foreign language shorthand acts as a means of recapitulation and reinforcement of the basic principles.

Spanish Teeline follows the style of French Teeline, by Ann Harvey. This was a conscious decision taken when writing the book. It was felt to be in the best interests of the students that their English, French and other language should have no anomalies. This would lessen the problem of alternative styles within one group of students and a possible resultant loss of speed.

The Spanish alphabet differs from English in that 'ch', 'll', 'ñ' are separate letters, and the letter 'w' is found only in words of foreign origin. For 'ch' we use the symbols for C and H: for the 'll' we use the single L symbol; for 'ñ' the basic symbol for N is used, and the accent is inserted if time permits.

Spanish spelling and pronunciation closely follow a given set of rules, and the spelling poses only a few minor problems. For example, 'c' is pronounced as 'th' before 'i' or 'e', and as 'k' before 'a', 'o', or 'u'; 'z' is always pronounced as 'th'. From the shorthand point of view the symbol for S is used for a medial 'z' where it is necessary, i.e. to avoid an ungainly outline. 'J' is always pronounced like the strong guttural 'ch' of *loch* (Scottish) and 'g' also has the same pronunciation when it is followed by an 'i' or an 'e'. At other times 'g' is pronounced as the English word *gate*.

Since the students generally have a sound knowledge of Spanish, they can mentally visualize the spelling of the word before recording the appropriate outlines. As Teeline is based on spelling to a great extent, then none of the above grammatical features has any great bearing on the manner in which the student deals with the words.

Prefixes and suffixes generally follow the same pattern as in English. For example, we use the English -MENT for the Spanish *mente/o/iento* (with slight variations): and -ATION English is also -*ción*. In the Spanish book we have sections for single word abbreviations, and also lists of commonly occurring phrases.

From our ten years' teaching experience in Spanish Teeline, we have found that it is relatively simple to adapt the English version into Spanish. We would go further to say that Teeline is readily adaptable to most foreign languages that share the alphabet.

The best opportunities for work in Spain exist in the large industrial cities where multinational companies often require secretaries with English as their native language.

In the UK there are many business concerns dealing with Spain and Central and South America. These include banks, fruit importers, travel firms, agricultural machinery and whisky companies. A number of Spanish businesses and banks also have branches in the UK.

Chapter 11 Intensive Courses

ANN DIX

Teeline lends itself well to intensive courses because it is possible to teach the theory quickly and to spend the maximum time available on speed-building. As in all shorthand systems it requires a good knowledge of English and this is particularly so as transcription relies heavily on context and students need to have a wide vocabulary.

The best way to conduct an intensive course is to work quickly through the theory, then immediately begin the cycle again with revision to drive home all the principles. I have found that some students at first resent the fast pace, but they accept the pressure once they realize they are making rapid progress and they can see for themselves how quickly they are acquiring a usable skill. For some students the system does not 'click' until the whole theory has been covered, but once this happens they catch up with the rest of the group quite quickly.

I have taught Teeline to the following company courses during the past twelve years:

block-release shorthand-typists' courses lasting 4 weeks for employees of all ages and educational standards;
secretarial courses lasting 16 weeks for post-A level school-leavers;
trainee news journalists' courses – Teeline as a note-taking medium with approximately 53 hours in which to teach the theory and reach a minimum speed of 60 w.p.m.

I use the same plan and material for teaching the theory for all three courses and vary the speed of learning according to the group. I allow more time for consolidation on the block-release course where levels of ability of the majority of students will be lower than on the other two courses. Once the theory-learning stage is completed, different material is used for speed and vocabulary-building according to the needs of the group.

I use the same method of presentation for all three courses based on James Hill's original lesson plans, but incorporating new theory which has been adopted since. The plan is as follows: basic alphabet and joining of letters; basic blends; TR and DR blends; CM, CN blends, PL blends, ICOM/ICON etc.; word beginnings; word endings; R indicating principle; days of the week, months, figures, abbreviations, etc.

Teeline's simplicity is its great attraction and I believe it is unnecessary to try to make it conform to methods of teaching used for traditional shorthand systems. There is no need to drill outlines illustrating theory principles to the point of boredom. The theory is so logical that for the most part students can understand *why* they are writing outlines as they are and therefore they learn quickly.

I introduce drills on common words, brief forms and simple joins on the first day of the course. Plenty of blackboard illustrations are given for each principle. I ask students to write Teeline outlines for longhand words illustrating each principle and drill with a few examples to enable students to get used to writing the new outlines. This is particularly helpful with blends, as some students find it difficult to form TN blends and F blends.

Students then read sentences, copy them from dictation, write them from dictation without reference to the original, read back from their notes and check their outlines with the original. I encourage the use of simple grouping at this stage, but do not worry unduly if students do not conform because not everyone takes readily to grouping and it is only really necessary for high-speed writing. I select material from the textbook and the workbooks for class work.

The following plans might be helpful to anyone embarking on an intensive course.

Block-release shorthand-typists' course
(4 weeks, 5 hours per day)

Mixed-ability group – mixed ages.
Aim: to achieve minimum speed of 60 w.p.m. on three-minute passages and equip students to take and transcribe office dictation, producing mailable documents. This plan is based on the following daily sessions: 1. 1 hour 10 mins; 2. 1 hour 30 mins; 3. 1 hour 15 mins; 4. 1 hour 5 mins.

Day 1:
1. Introduction to system – history – inventor – how it is written – how the amount of writing is reduced. Letters of the alphabet – notes on their uses, how to write them and the abbreviated forms that the letters represent. Practise writing letters and drill special forms. Practise joining letters together – use very simple words.
2. Letters T and D: disjoins after R and upward L; disjoins following one another. Letter S – direction of writing. Letter X for EX. Letters I, Y and OY. Special use of I indicator for -ING. 'Soft' C. Words ending -AY. Read and copy outlines to illustrate all theory covered so far – students suggest words for outlines.
3. Revise letters of alphabet and vowels. Notes on vowels – when to use full vowels and when to use indicators – plenty of examples. Give students longhand words to write in Teeline – put on blackboard for checking.
4. Notes on use of double vowels (vowel blends). Use of vowel indicators as word endings -ANG, -ENG, -ING, -ONG, -UNG and extension to

-ANC, etc. Common word drill. Give words for students to put into Teeline for homework.

Day 2 :
1. Check homework. Revise alphabet. Re-read exercise on words used previous day. Additional practice on joining letters – vowel between B and consonants, R and M, position of T and D. Common word drill.
2. Reading, copying and dictation of simple sentences – drill difficult and distinguishing outlines first. Basic blends: F blends, N blends, R blends, X blends, V blends, PB blend. Drills – words to illustrate use of blends; students write these in Teeline – blackboard outlines for checking.
3. Reading, copying and dictation practice on sentences illustrating basic blends.
4. Drill on brief forms. Reading, copying practice on theory covered so far.

Day 3 :
1. Revision of alphabet. Dictation of exercise read in last session on previous day. TR and DR blends, THR, TN and DN, TRN and DRN – drills.
2. Special use of N for -TION, -CIAN, -SION, etc. Read and copy sentences illustrating TR and DR blends.
3. Re-read and dictate above exercise. Drill common words.
4. Dictation of simple passage – practise outlines first. This gives students tremendous encouragement – they can see that they already have a usable knowledge of the system. Dictate the passage at approximately 15 w.p.m., get them to read back from their notes, put passage on blackboard for them to check their notes, then re-dictate at 15 w.p.m. and repeat at 20. Notes on joining simple common words: words followed by *the, have* and *is, I am, to be,* etc.

Day 4 :
1. Revise TR and DR blends. Introduce CM/CN blends and -NCE ending.
2. Read and dictate sentences illustrating new blends. General passage for dictation – prepare by reading, copying and drilling. Common word list – a few outlines to be learned and drilled per day during rest of course on cyclic plan.
3. Revise CM/CN blends. Introduce PL blend and ICOM/ICON.
4. Reading, copying and dictation on all new blends.

Day 5 :
1. Revise all blends. Recap on vowel blends. Reading and dictation for revision.

2. Theory test. Distinguishing outlines – to be learned and drilled during rest of course on cyclic plan. Introduce word beginnings. Reading, copying and dictation on word beginnings.

3. Reading and dictation on theory covered so far. Phrase and common word drills.

4. Revision of ICOM/ICON and -NCE – re-read sentences using these blends – dictation.

Day 6:

1. New week, so revise alphabet! Common word drill. Revise word beginnings. Re-read sentences used previously for word beginnings. Introduce word endings, -ABLE, etc.

2. Introduce rest of word endings. Reading, copying exercise.

3. Re-read exercise used previous session – dictate. Common word drill.

4. Dictation: common word passage – prepare in usual way by drilling outlines and groups – dictate at approximately 20 w.p.m. – read back – blackboard for checking – re-dictate at 30 w.p.m. – short sections repeated at higher speeds if possible.

Day 7:

1. Revise word endings. Revise word beginnings. Reading, copying and dictation practice for word beginnings and endings.

2. Common word drill. Introduce R indicating principle. Reading, copying and dictation.

3. Dictation: prepare passage – dictate at 30 w.p.m. – repeat at 40 and 50.

4. Introduce: Days of week, months, figures, per cent, abbreviations. Drills and exercise on above.

Total time spent on first theory lessons = 35 hours.

New learning of theory could be completed in 25 hours, but as students attend all day, allowance has to be made for the fact that there is a limit to the amount of new learning that can be done in one day, and the time has to be divided between new learning and working on the familiar, with dictation practice now and again to alleviate the pressure. If students were attending for only 2 hours per day one could push them harder and achieve the 25-hour target for theory learning.

The remainder of the course is spent as follows: revision of theory, speed-building, dictation and typed transcription of letters, memos, reports, etc.

Three-minute RSA standard speed tests are given at the end of the course with 2 per cent error allowance for pass.

Secretarial course

(16 weeks; 25 hours' theory, 75 hours' speed-building)
Post A level students.

Aim: to train students to be junior secretaries with minimum shorthand
speed of 80 w.p.m. (Those with real ability can achieve 90–100.)

Lesson 1 (2 hours 30 mins):
Introduction to system – history – inventor – how the amount of writing
is reduced. Letters of the alphabet – notes on their uses, how to write
them and the abbreviated forms that the letters represent. Practise
writing letters and drill short forms. Practise joining letters together –
use very simple words. Letters T and D: disjoins after R and upward L;
disjoins following one another. Letter S – direction of writing – 'Soft' C.
Letter X for EX. Letters I, Y, and OY – words ending in -AY.

Lesson 2 (1 hour 30 mins):
Revision of alphabet. Consolidation – reading outlines and suggesting
words. Notes on vowels – when to use full vowels and when to use
indicators – plenty of examples. -ING endings.

Lesson 3 (1 hour 30 mins):
Reading exercise – read and copy outlines, suggesting words. Additional
practice in joining letters and for words containing upward L and R
followed by T and D. Facility drill on common words and simple joins.
Homework: words to put into Teeline illustrating all theory covered.

Lesson 4 (1 hour 30 mins):
Check homework. Basic blends: F blend, N blend, R blend, X blend, V
blend, PB blend. Reading, copying and dictation on blends. Common
word list – a few outlines to be drilled each day on cyclic plan. Dictation
of simple passage – practise outlines first. Dictate passage at
approximately 15 w.p.m. – students read from their notes – passage on
blackboard for checking – students check – re-dictate at same speed,
then repeat at 20 w.p.m. Homework: outlines for words containing all
theory covered so far.

Lesson 5 (1 hour):
Check homework. Common word drill. Revision – reading and dictation
on basic blends.

Lesson 6 (1 hour 30 mins):
TR and DR blends, THR, TN and DN, TRN and DRN – drills. N for
-TION, etc. Reading, copying and dictation on blends.

Lesson 7 (1 hour 30 mins):
Revise TR and DR blends. Common word drill. Introduce CM/CN blends. Reading, copying and dictation on blends.

Lesson 8 (1 hour 30 mins):
Revise CM/CN blends. Common word drill. Joining simple common words – simple grouping. PL blend followed by reading and copying.

Lesson 9 (1 hour 30 mins):
Revise PL blend – reading and dictation on blend. Revise all other blends: N, R, WR, MR, LR. Reading and dictation practice on above. Common word drill.

Lesson 10 (1 hour 30 mins):
Common word drill. Quick revision of letter S – 'Soft' C. Introduce ICOM/ICON, etc. and -NCE ending. Reading, copying and dictation. Theory test: longhand passage to be written in Teeline.

Lesson 11 (1 hour 30 mins):
Return marked test – discuss – re-dictate. Common word drill. Word beginnings: reading, copying and dictation. Distinguishing outlines – drill some each day on cyclic plan.

Lesson 12 (1 hour):
Revise word beginnings. Common words and distinguishing outlines drills.

Lesson 13 (1 hour):
Word endings: -ANG, -ANC, -ABLE, etc.; -SHL; -OLOGY; -WARD; -MENT – plenty of examples – drills – followed by reading, copying and dictation. Common word drill.

Lesson 14 (1 hour):
Rest of word endings: -GRAPH; -SELF; -FUL; -FULNESS; -LESSNESS; -ARITY; -ORITY; -INGLY – plenty of examples – drills – followed by reading, copying and dictation. Common word drill and distinguishing outlines drill.

Lesson 15 (1 hour 30 mins):
Revision of word endings. Additional reading, copying and dictation practice on word beginnings and endings. Common word and distinguishing outlines drills.

Lesson 16 (1 hour):
Introduce R indicating principle. Reading, copying and dictation practice on above. Common words and distinguishing outlines drills.

Lesson 17 (1 hour):
Revise R indicating principle. Common word and distinguishing outlines drills.

Lesson 18 (1 hour 30 mins):
Introduce: days of week, months, figures, per cent, abbreviations. Drills and exercise on above. Common word and distinguishing outlines drills.

Total time spent on first theory lessons = 25 hours.
This plan allows plenty of time for consolidation of each principle. The learning time can be reduced by allowing less time for reading, copying and dictation. I have taught basic theory in twelve 1-hour lessons, but this is insufficient time to allow students to acquire confidence in handling the system or for a reasonable vocabulary to be mastered. Lessons can be adapted to 1-hour sessions if fewer examples are worked and shorter exercises are used. Five to ten minutes' daily drilling is sufficient for common words and distinguishing outlines.

The remainder of the course is spent on speed-building with revision of theory included in the first few lessons if required. Typed transcription is encouraged from an early stage: as soon as students have mastered the keyboard sufficiently I dictate simple untimed letters for typed transcription, usually during the fourth week of the course.

Three-minute RSA standard speed tests are given at the end of the course with 2 per cent error allowance for a pass.

Trainee news journalists' course
(8 days followed by six weekly sessions of approximately $2\frac{1}{4}$ hours each) Graduates.

Aim: to equip trainees with a note-taking medium. Fifty-three hours allocated for theory and speed-building up to 60 w.p.m. This plan is based on the following daily sessions: 1. 1 hour 10 mins; 2. 1 hour 30 mins; 3. 1 hour 15 mins; 4. 1 hour.

Day 1:
1. Introduction – shortening devices, silent letters, etc. Alphabet – practise writing. Joining vowels and consonants.
2. Letters T and D. L and R after T and D. Positioning of S, intersection of X, I for Y. Special forms as per alphabet. Reading, copying basic outlines.
3. Revision of basics. Vowel blends. Upward L after H, P, G. Vowels used to facilitate outline with two S's, between B and other consonants. OY, ING, ANG and extension to INC, ANC.
4. 'Soft' C, simple downward L. Longhand words illustrating theory covered in last two sessions; students suggest Teeline outlines for these

words. Drill simple special forms and groups. Reading and writing
practice. Homework: Twenty words illustrating principles – students
write Teeline outlines.

Day 2:
1. Check homework words and discuss any queries and problems.
Introduce basic blends – give examples – drills.
2. Reading and writing exercise – keep note on distinguishing and
special outlines. Words containing blends – students write outlines.
3. TR and DR blends and -TION. Examples – drills. Groups using
there. Examples – drills.
4. Reading and writing practice on TR and DR blends.

Day 3:
1. Revise basic and TR and DR blends. Words containing blends –
students write outlines.
2. CM/CN blends, N blends and -NCE – examples – drills. Groups
with *have* and *is*. Reading, copying and dictation.
3. PL blend, ICOM/ICON, etc. – examples – drills. Words containing
new blends – students write outlines.
4. Reading, copying and dictation practice on the above.

Day 4:
Revision of all blends. Examples and students suggest outlines for words.
2. Reading, copying and dictation practice on all blends.
3. Word beginnings – examples – drills. Words containing word
beginnings – students write outlines.
4. Reading, copying and dictation practice on word beginnings.

Day 5:
1. Revise word beginnings. Reading and writing practice.
2. Give half the word endings – plenty of examples – drills. Words
containing endings – students write outlines.
3. Give other half of word endings – examples – drills. Words
containing endings – students write outlines.
4. Reading and writing practice for word endings. Homework: revision
and learning of word endings.

Day 6:
1. Revise all theory learned so far. Short theory word test.
2. Reading and writing practice for word beginnings and endings.
3. Introduce R indicating principle – examples – drills. Words containing
R principle – students write outlines.
4. Reading and writing practice on the above. Homework: words with
the R principle.

Day 7:
1. Revise R indicating principle – reading and writing practice.
2. Groups – work and read and write exercise.
3. Revision of all theory – reading, dictation practice.
4. Revision of all theory as above.

Day 8:
1. Word groupings. Dictation of unseen matter, preparing difficult words, phrases – increase speed.
2. Dictation on blends (re-using exercises previously worked) and check outlines – increase speed.
3. Dictate previously used exercise on word beginnings – check outlines – increase speed.
4. Dictate previously used exercise on word endings – check outlines – increase speed.

Six half-day sessions:
Consolidation of theory, work on phrases and vocabulary. Speed-building. Topical items from the newspapers and bulletins from a newsroom where available. Homework: an article in shorthand for preparation for the following week or writing an article from a newspaper in Teeline.

Owing to the limited time available to absorb the theory it is essential for some homework to be done during the first eight days. If time is short, the instructor can read exercises with the group, or students can work in pairs as this speeds up the reading process. It often helps the slower student. Students can be encouraged to ask for outlines for difficult words which they have noticed in the day's news – often a hair-raising experience for the instructor, but it generates a good discussion on theory!

If higher speeds are required then proportional additional time can be allocated for further sessions: 10 hours per ten words per minute is the recognized standard.

Speed-building for intensive courses
Speed-building sessions can be conducted in the same way as for other shorthand systems. Difficult words should be drilled before dictation and students reminded about outlines for groups and special forms that occur in the passage.

I find that Teeline students are less inclined to ask for outlines. If an unfamiliar word causes hesitation during dictation they can usually work out an outline for themselves once the dictation has ended and they have time to think. They may merely ask for confirmation that what they have written is acceptable. This is a pleasant experience for the teacher as one feels less like a walking dictionary than one does when teaching other systems!

Students often suggest alternative ways of writing outlines and providing they conform to the basic principles of the system this is perfectly acceptable. I find these suggestions encourage class discussion and quite often students suggest some excellent ideas for grouping which have not appeared in the textbooks. Classes are highly motivated and happy.

Chapter 12 Teeline in Journalism

I Teaching Postgraduate Students
GEORGE HILL

Elsewhere in this book other teachers write about their experiences of teaching Teeline to either graduates on commercial courses or trainee newspaper journalists. My topic is teaching Teeline to graduates who are not yet journalists but are hoping to take up eventual employment in the communications media – newspapers, magazines, news agencies, radio or television.

The students

The students are graduates in a number of disciplines, from philosophy to chemistry, politics to history, languages to mathematics. They are mostly aged 21–23 with the occasional mature student. The class size is about thirty, usually with a few more males than females. The majority are unmarried. Students occasionally include an overseas student from the USA, Africa, India or the Far East.

The Diploma course

The academic and practical content of the Diploma course prepares the students for work in both print and broadcast media. Areas of study include reporting, editing, feature writing, interviewing, the history and social functions of the media, the law as it affects the journalist, local and central government.

The Teeline component

For Teeline there are 120 hours' tuition over the full academic year (October to June, inclusive). As far as possible, there is one 1-hour lesson each day to a total of 100 hours by the end of the second term. The remaining 20 hours are 'dotted around' in the final term. The target is 100 w.p.m. for four minutes, examined by the National Council for the Training of Journalists.

The first term

It is rare for any student to encounter a serious problem. One of my first tasks is to explode some of the myths and misconceptions that are brought to the classroom by students. I normally do this by holding a fifteen-minute question and answer session during the first lesson. Yes, shorthand can be difficult, but Teeline is easy. Yes, regular practice is necessary. No, some of my best students have been (and possibly still are) left-handed. Yes, Teeline adapts easily to many other languages. It is basically orthographic, not phonetic. It can be written with pen or pencil. No, you do not translate it, you transcribe it. Yes, there is a correct way to sit and a correct way to use a notebook. (Demonstrate.) Yes, regular attendance is vital. Yes, we have a library of practice tapes from 30–120 w.p.m. Do not talk about Teeline 'lectures'. Call them lessons or sessions. Think of Teeline as handwriting minus its non-essential elements.

The theory is split into twenty-five modules, each of which can be taught in 1 hour with ample time for consolidation through exercises and/or dictation. The Teeline alphabet, for instance, is divided into three units, the first containing the letters G, H, M, N, R, S and T. After demonstrating these letters (stressing their derivation from longhand and the direction in which each of them is written) I show how some of them are joined to make words – *goes*, *home* or *near*. I then ask the students to write a few words – *them*, *gone*, *rise* or *managers*. With graduates, this kind of creative or 'discovery' learning is far more effective than spoon-feeding. The single-letter words *go*, *he*, *me/may*, *and*, *are* and *to* are also taught as part of this unit.

After 10 hours, or 2 weeks' tuition, a progress check is carried out. This consists of 100 words to be put into Teeline in half an hour. At this stage, only two blends (FR and HV) and two word endings (-ING and -ABLE) have been taught. Having marked the progress check, I now have sufficient material for an entire lesson to be devoted to revision.

The students are now ready to borrow a '30 tape' consisting of passages that can be written without the application of any Teeline principles not yet learnt. Speed targets, starting with 40 w.p.m. after week five and rising by 10 w.p.m. per week, are set for the rest of the term. In the final week the students are tested at 70 for four minutes and 80 for two minutes. The majority pass on both tests. I waste my breath exhorting them to practise over the Christmas vacation.

The second term

At the beginning of the second term, it may be found that two students have decided that journalism is not for them. The remainder rejoin the course minus 10 w.p.m. I then spend two weeks pulling them back to 70 and 80 – and reminding them of points of theory obliterated from their memories by weeks of Christmas celebration. Attendance falls as the term proceeds. They stick on the 80 plateau. They get influenza or have to interview some local dignitary, finish a project, attend their grandmother's funeral in Inverness. They get thrown out of their lodgings. The weather is bad. There is a bus/rail strike. They apply for jobs and go for interviews in Shropshire.

When they sit the NCTJ exam (four minutes at 100) at the end of term, the average attendance is 94 out of a possible 100 hours. About one-third of them pass. I waste my breath exhorting them to practise over the Easter vacation.

The third term

When the third term begins they start with a 'TV fortnight' so it is 7 weeks since I last saw them. One student has left the course, having obtained a post. Also absent from my sessions are most of those who passed at 100 w.p.m. They rest on their laurels. Neither shall I see much of those who have opted for a career in radio or television rather than newspapers. They do not need shorthand – or so I am told. I now do 1, 2 or 3 hours a week for eight, ten or twelve students. They take the examination several times, most of them getting through before the term ends. A few attempt higher speeds. A handful pass at 110 for four minutes and a couple at 120 for four minutes. In one glorious year, two students passed at 130 for four minutes.

Reflections

This kind of course presents insoluble problems for the Teeline teacher. Unlike in-company training courses, there is not the ultimate sanction of dismissal for failing to reach the required standard and the self-discipline needed for progress beyond 80 w.p.m. is not easy to cultivate on a course that has an essentially academic atmosphere. The long breaks between terms are particularly damaging to the impetus of the students' progress up the speed ladder. The same – if not better – results would be achieved with the same number of hours' tuition given over 20 consecutive weeks.

Then there is the gradual development among the students of the feeling that shorthand is an intrusion on the rest of the course. Having a somewhat academic bent of mind myself, I can understand that learning the theory is, especially for graduates, by far the most interesting and stimulating part of the proceedings: even so, the lack of sustained effort and dwindling attendance in the last two terms are depressing.

I try to maintain interest throughout the course by the use of dictation passages that are informative, amusing or concerned with journalism. Newspapers, magazines, short stories and poetry – all are grist to my mill. I also read scores of past exam papers. For the most part, transcription is set as homework, but plenty of reading back is done in class. Incidentally, I remember one student who refused to read back in class because she was 'poetic'! Not surprisingly, she never passed 'the 100'. Thankfully, such problems of temperament are rare.

For the most part, the students read back or transcribe their own Teeline, but they are occasionally asked to decipher a classmate's notes. This is a good way of introducing some variety into a lesson and they take great delight in pointing out each other's mistakes and discussing alternative outlines.

The teacher's qualities

In addition to such obvious qualities as patience and resilience, the teacher who wishes to remain sane throughout this kind of course should possess the following assets:

1. an appreciation of the ways in which Teeline principles can be extended and adapted by the intelligent writer;
2. the ability to recognize and accept viable alternative outlines;
3. a wide general knowledge;
4. a fair grasp of what journalism is all about;
5. a high degree of competence in the English language.

Finally, a word of advice. Do not assume that a graduate is bound to have all the qualities needed to become a successful Teeliner. In my experience, graduates are like the little girl in the nursery rhyme: when they are good they are very, very good; but when they are bad . . .

II Teaching on In-Company Schemes
JEAN CLARKSON

Success in shorthand is largely a matter of motivation and here the in-company schemes have a big advantage. By the time the trainees start on an in-company course they will have gone through a process of aptitude tests and interviews and the Teeline tutor has virtually a hand-picked class to mould.

It must be remembered that they are not students in the usual sense, as they are employees who are paid a weekly wage while undergoing their training. Not only do their editors release them for the duration of the course but their newspapers pay out a lot of money to finance the training scheme. In these circumstances editors are entitled to expect good results.

It is made quite clear to trainees from the first day of the course that their jobs as reporters depend on the amount of effort they put into the course, and failure could mean that there will be no job for them when the course is finished.

The in-company training schemes are accountable, and this is the secret of their success. On most courses regular reports are sent to editors to chart the progress of the trainees. Sometimes editors may feel it necessary to call in a young reporter if they are not happy with the progress being made.

In-company schemes do not have the college problem of trainees missing lectures. If this happened without a good reason being given there would be a quick telephone call to their newspapers.

Courses vary in length from company to company, but a rough guide is a 14-week course for graduates and up to 20 weeks for school-leavers. The two groups usually have separate courses and most companies aim to run both courses in one academic year. Shorthand is slotted into a busy timetable which includes law, public administration, and use of journalistic English, coupled with practical journalism. At the end of the course the trainee is expected to pass examinations in all these subjects set by the National Council for the Training of Journalists.

In the case of shorthand a minimum speed of 100 w.p.m. on a four-minute passage is required, but many trainees reach higher speeds with Teeline. A reporter needs an extensive shorthand vocabulary and can be expected to cover anything from a flower show opening to a major disaster. This is reflected in the test passages which are acknowledged to be of more than average difficulty. The passage is always part of a speech and can be anything from a coroner's summing up at an inquest to a Member of Parliament addressing the House of Commons; from a mayor opening a new block of flats for the elderly to a company managing director announcing redundancies among the work-force.

Some trainee journalists take a lot of convincing that shorthand is not an academic subject that you can 'read up'. It is essentially a skill and it takes daily practice to become proficient. It comes as something of a shock when they realize the amount of effort needed to learn shorthand, reach a speed of 100, and maintain it for four minutes. However, they have the advantage of a good knowledge of the English language, which is an asset to anyone learning shorthand as teachers of mixed-ability groups will appreciate.

If a target of 100 w.p.m. is to be reached during the course, a lot of thought and planning has to go into the timetable. The speed is not achieved in the space of a few weeks without a lot of hard work and dedication on the part of the tutor and the trainee, and it is essential to introduce a sense of urgency from the outset.

Trainees must be convinced of the need for shorthand and that they will not get far in their careers without it. Having established that the reporters with the best shorthand get the best assignments, target dates should be set *and adhered to* for the completion of the theory and lower speeds. If a trainee is getting behind, most company courses have a library of speed tapes that can be borrowed for private study. You cannot allow the slowest in the group to dictate the speed of progress.

One thing that is certain on in-company courses is that every minute counts and the trainees know that 100 per cent effort is expected from them for the whole time. This may sound very high-powered and pressurized but the trainees generally respond and are encouraged by their speed of progress with Teeline. Obviously it is necessary from time to time to introduce a few light-hearted pieces to break the tension.

The number of tuition hours varies from course to course but it is significant that the best results are not achieved on those courses with the greatest number of hours. Quite the opposite seems to be the case. It is possible with Teeline to reach the 100 w.p.m. target in 100 hours with able students, but even average trainees can achieve this in 100–150 hours and they do so regularly. If the course is spread over too many hours it becomes counter-productive and boredom sets in.

Teeline is best approached with the intention of halving the number of hours and a good teacher takes care to see that that aim is achieved.

Most in-company courses aim to complete the theory in the first 2 or 3 weeks. The Teeline work-load is not great compared with other systems and there is no benefit in stretching out the theory period any longer than 20–25 hours. Parkinson's Law applies to Teeline, in that work will always last as long as the time available for it. The sooner the theory is dispensed with the better, for there is no greater tonic for a student than to make an early start on simple sentences. This is one of the great advantages of Teeline.

Once the theory is mastered and speed-building starts, daily lessons are essential. Most schemes work on the basis of short but frequent lessons and this seems to be the secret of success. Ideally no lesson should last longer than 1 hour – 45 minutes is better – and there should be one lesson in the morning and one in the afternoon. One company that produces consistently good results prides itself on lessons lasting no longer than half an hour, but these may be difficult to fit into a busy timetable geared to longer teaching periods.

It is only when the trainees reach the point where they hear and see everything in Teeline that real progress is made. A useful guide to work to is: 50 hours' tuition – 50 w.p.m.; 60 hours' tuition – 60 w.p.m.; 70 hours' tuition – 70 w.p.m., and so on.

Not all trainees will be able to maintain this rate of progress but many do so without any trouble and these inspire the rest of the group. It sometimes takes longer to make the transition from 90 to 100 and extra time should be allowed for this when planning the course. A hundred w.p.m. on passages of two or three minutes presents no difficulty. The problem arises when they have to maintain the speed for four minutes. This extra minute inevitably proves a stumbling block and it takes a great deal of determination, stamina and good humour to conquer the four-minute barrier.

Discipline is essential on these short courses and trainees are expected to work from 9 a.m. to 5 p.m. After the first few weeks they go out to courts, council meetings, etc. and are told to use their shorthand even if it means taking down a mixture of longhand and shorthand. Their notebooks should be inspected to make sure that they are doing this.

The teaching of shorthand must be related to the creative business of learning to be a journalist and the sooner they put it to practical use the better.

Editor's note: the NCTJ examination now consists of one 4-minute passage in 2-minute sections, with an interval of 30 seconds between the two.

Chapter 13 The Speed Class

RUTH FRYER

The object of the speed class is to teach students to write legible shorthand at a fast speed so that it can be read back accurately and quickly. This may sound like a truism but it is important that teachers bear this objective in mind from the beginning of their courses, as their students will not achieve their full potential unless they are taught proper methods.

From the first moment that 'writing faster' is mentioned – and that will be in the early stages – good writing habits should be established. For this you need a good writing position, seated comfortably at a desk, one hand holding the pen lightly so that it will 'flow' across the page. The other hand should steady the shorthand pad (and not hold the head) so that the page can be turned quickly.

Other factors that affect speed acquisition are:

The ability to think quickly: (a) immediate recall of outlines so that they can be written without hesitation. This, of course, assumes a thorough knowledge of Teeline theory; (b) to shorten outlines just sufficiently to suggest the correct word. This is an additional skill to be learned and depends to a certain extent on intelligence and a good working knowledge of English.

Concentration on the task in hand, immediately before dictation as well as during it, and the exclusion of outside distractions.

Self-motivation: the will to succeed even though a 'plateau' or speed block has been reached.

Successful increase in speed: success is necessary to build confidence and this can be done with passages containing easy vocabulary with many word-groups.

Psychological advantage of writing Teeline: the freedom of writing Teeline eliminates the guilt feelings of not writing the 'correct' outline. It is not a crime if a longer or shorter outline is written than that suggested in the textbook. 'Something for everything' is a very good rule (in other words, an outline or part of an outline) for every word dictated. A gap in the notes indicates nothing, whereas the first letter(s) of a word can give a clue when read in context. The urge to stop and think must be resisted if one is to progress to the next 10 w.p.m. of speed.

A wide vocabulary is necessary if one is to write shorthand at speed. An unusual word will cause uncertainty and momentarily break concentration. Students should be encouraged to read widely to limit this difficulty.

When learning the theory, passages which apply to particular rules are dictated at increasing speeds, but I find it better to start a true speed class when the whole of the theory has been learned. This enables a wider vocabulary to be used in dictation passages. By that time the class can be divided into slower and faster groups. If it is possible to share classes, then the students can be arranged to include a fast group, but the teacher needs to be well organized to get the best results.

Boredom inhibits speed, so a variety of approaches is necessary to keep interest alive. As an amount of repetition in dictation and reading back is inevitable this must be broken up, and I try various methods.

One is the preparation of a passage before dictation by extracting words and groupings, and asking the class to write their own immediate response to them before I give my version on the blackboard. Then they compare their outlines with mine to see which they prefer. This need not take long, and some very good shortenings are produced in this way which are liked by some students but not by others. After that comes dictation and reading back either individually or in chorus. Afterwards there is a discussion of groupings and any other difficulties before re-dictating at a faster speed.

It is important to remember that if one student only is reading the passage, s/he may be nervous and hesitant. The temptation to prompt by the teacher and the class must be resisted. The student should be encouraged to read ahead, as the context of the passage will often give a clue to the missing words. In fact, a good 'context' training is to give sentences for transcription with certain missing words to be supplied by the student, with or without a list of words.

A variation on the theme of reading back is to divide the class into groups, number them, and when one group stumbles, call out the number of another to continue the passage.

Another method is that of 'cold' dictation, i.e. without preparation. After dictation, outlines are given for any words that caused difficulty and during reading back attention is drawn to difficult words and groupings. Then there is re-dictation at the same speed, or faster if preferred.

Short passages can be used to promote speed with easy vocabulary, difficult vocabulary or mainly word-groupings, and dictated at ever-increasing speeds until it is obvious that the maximum speed has been reached. These passages can be read back at intervals. At the end students note the speed at which their outlines began to deteriorate and try to do better the next time.

Longer passages of easy or difficult vocabulary, and amusing or serious content, can be used either with or without preparation. The method here is to dictate for half a minute at a higher speed than the group can manage, with a short break for the slower ones to catch up (usually only a few seconds) before continuing in the same way throughout the passage. The whole passage is then read back with a discussion of difficulties or better ways to write words.

The passage is then re-dictated in one-minute bursts in the same way, and the final dictation is of the whole passage without a break. Reading back can take place in the next lesson when the notes are 'cold' and memory is receding.

This method can be varied by dividing the passage in half with only one break, or dictating the whole passage at an easy speed for the group to give time for thought. Discussion of outlines can come at the end of the dictation or the reading back and then there is re-dictation at a higher speed. As examinations approach, past papers may increasingly be used for this purpose.

Passages should be read back or transcribed (either by hand or typewritten) and this is essential when preparing for examinations, so passages dictated in the speed class can well be used for transcription. It is inevitable that shorthand style deteriorates as the students press for speed so it is advisable that occasionally they should be encouraged to write clear outlines. This can be done after transcription by writing the same passage in a good shorthand style.

The introduction of new technology into secretarial courses has meant less time to spend on shorthand, so one way to get over the difficulty of acquiring speed is to set up a cassette tape library of different speeds, e.g. 50 repeated at 60, 60 repeated at 70 and so on. Students borrow the tapes for both homework and classwork. To take full advantage of such a library it is necessary for students to have cassette players at home and for adequate numbers of players to be available in class.

In the beginning stages, if all students are working on a particular tape (say 50/60), the longhand of the first two or three passages could be given for preparation before starting the tape work and then at the end of a week the passages are dictated in class at 60/70.

If it is not possible to set up a tape library then all is not lost, for public libraries usually have some shorthand speed records or tapes, or if not they will obtain them. Commercially produced tapes are also available.

Over the years there have been nearly 500 shorthand systems. Fortunately for the teacher who is battling to increase speed, not all of them are written today, but there are six systems (including Teeline) that are currently on offer at our educational institutions. It is possible, therefore, that the speed class could contain students who write other systems – hopefully not all of them! You are fortunate if the class speed is uniform, but it could be that the speeds range from 60–120 +. In this event it is going to be hard work, but not an impossible task.

Good class organization is essential. For the best results, try to install the class in a room containing cassette players and use shorthand speed tapes. Divide the class in half by speed, say 60–90 and 100–120 +. In a

2- to 3-hour day release or evening class, half the time would be spent with one part while the other part takes dictation from speed tapes. Passages are prepared by the extraction of words and word groups.

If the teacher is familiar with more than one system then the board should be divided into sections and the outlines written accordingly. If there are still students writing systems not known to the teacher, then the students should have dictionaries appropriate to the systems to give some guidance.

A variation is to give the whole group the longhand of some of the passages to be dictated so that these can be written in their own system. Discussion can follow and then the passage is dictated.

It is important that transcription plays its part in a speed class and so periodically, instead of leaving transcription for homework, the time normally apportioned for cassette work should be used for this.

In many colleges it is quite usual to find that the speed groups of full-time secretarial students contain writers of several systems. It is a great help if the teacher is familiar with more than one system, thus increasing the confidence of students – an important ingredient in the acquisition of shorthand speed.

You may feel that the teacher needs to be a 'superbeing' – not so, just well organized!

Chapter 14 Teaching Evening Classes

DOROTHY BOWYER

Taking an evening class is quite different from any other form of teaching. In a college or school, students will usually be in the same age group and at about the same level of achievement. An evening class, however, may include school-leavers, young office workers, housewives, shop workers wishing to qualify for office work, old-age pensioners seeking a new interest in life, as well as a sprinkling of businessmen and women, and trainee journalists.

All these people will have one factor in common – they will be eager to learn. Of course, the range of ability will be very wide. Young people who have not achieved very much at school may be found mingling with graduates, so learning speeds will vary enormously. This means, then, that the problem of arousing and maintaining interest is greater, and that one has to keep the more-able students happily occupied while, at the same time, helping those who are slower to learn.

The first evening will be occupied for some time with writing up the register, which to begin with will be a temporary one. A list of those who have enrolled for the class is usually issued so that attendance can be checked. Inevitably there will be late enrolments to be dealt with, and it will be necessary to make sure that students have come to the right room. Probably some will arrive very late, having mistaken the room number. It is important, however, to make a start on the subject teaching as soon as possible, otherwise students will go away with feelings of disappointment. Students beginning a new subject at evening class are usually eager to get started, and it is up to the evening class teacher to nurture this initial enthusiasm.

It is wise to take a supply of paper and pencils or ballpoint pens to the first class. It is surprising how many people go along to a shorthand class taking no writing implement and no paper on which to write!

Deal with the preliminaries quickly, and then talk for a short time about shorthand systems in general and Teeline in particular. Students who have tried unsuccessfully to learn other systems will be delighted to hear that it is so easy. At this point I explain that when writing shorthand one first reduces the words to 'skeletons' or 'outlines', by eliminating unnecessary letters and writing only what is essential for accurate transcription of the word. To illustrate this principle one might write a simple sentence on the chalkboard, reducing the words in this way. Such a sentence might read *I shd lk t se u tmrw*. The group will generally have no difficulty in deciphering this. Then write the sentence in Teeline so that they may see what it looks like. Write a few more words and sentences in longhand, reducing them to outlines as before, and then get the students to try it. Once this principle has been assimilated the class is ready to proceed.

Write the Teeline alphabet on the chalkboard, explaining how each sign is derived from its longhand form. Take care to form the signs clearly, and explain that your handwriting style may be different from that of others, so the slope of such letters as P and H may also be different. Ask the class to copy out the alphabet, taking care to write very neatly in their normal handwriting size, and to practise this for a time.

While they are doing this, it is possible to go round to each student and complete the registration details while looking at their work and discussing it with them. Try to get them to develop a good writing style from the start, before any bad habits can develop. By the time the paper work is completed, they will be ready for the next step, which is the use of some of the letters of the alphabet as words, such as *a, be, to, very*, etc.

Next, show how to join the letters to form words. Write a few simple words in Teeline, such as *odd, many, bag, let, knob*, etc. on the board. The students read them aloud and then copy them. From this, proceed to a simple sentence, such as *Teeline is easy to read and easy to write.*

This may seem to be covering a good deal in the first lesson, but the aim is to let the students see how easy the system is. Emphasize that everything will be revised later, and that this speed of presentation will not be maintained throughout the course.

If there is time, ask each student's name and write it on the board for them. Students, particularly the younger element, like to see their names written in Teeline, and take great pleasure in decorating their notebooks with the outlines. It also helps the teacher to start learning their names!

This is usually as much as can be done on the first evening. Before the students leave, ask them to make certain that they know the alphabet and the special words for the next lesson. I also ask those who have not done so to provide themselves with the textbook and, of course, a shorthand notebook.

It is advisable to work out exactly what is to be taught each week. Before classes begin, go through the textbook, dividing up the theory according to the number of weeks in the session. Allow time for revision and for speed-building. Decide upon the objectives for the course and then for individual lessons.

Always go into class knowing what you are going to teach and how you intend to go about it. Keep a 'workbook' for each class. This is an ordinary exercise book in which brief details of each lesson are recorded, together with items that need additional work or revision, homework marks, examination entries, and so on.

At first it is difficult to gauge just how much work will be covered in an evening, and it is advisable to have supplementary material in case the lesson is completed sooner than anticipated. Set some homework each week and make a point of taking it in for checking. Students become very discouraged if the teacher neglects to look at their work regularly. For homework, set exercises from the textbook, or a transcription exercise when they have progressed further.

At the second meeting of the class, check that the students have done their homework by dictating the alphabet to them several times, with pauses for checking. Start slowly and gradually increase the speed until they can write without hesitation. Do the same with the special forms. Remind them about reducing words to skeletons and dictate a few easy words for them to write in Teeline, checking the outlines from the board.

This lesson should be mainly on the joining of strokes. It is essential that the students should understand clearly how to join the strokes and extra time spent on this is well worth while. Go round and look at their work, giving individual help where necessary.

Evening class students usually have only one lesson a week, so full use must be made of the time available. Plan the lesson carefully. It is best to proceed from the known to the unknown, so that the first part of the lesson should be a brief recap of the previous week's work. Encourage students to ask questions about any problems that may have arisen, either with their homework or in class. After the brief revision period, introduce a new principle.

I usually follow the tried and tested method of explaining the theory, writing examples on the board, asking the class to copy them, and they then write words, using the new rule, from dictation. I write the outlines on the board for them to check. Quite often I prepare a 'gapped' hand-out, which explains the theory with examples and has spaces for the student to complete. These are particularly useful in the early stages.

Towards the end of each lesson students are asked to do some writing in Teeline at their own speed. This may take the form of four or five sentences or a short continuous passage which I write in longhand on the chalkboard. They like to discuss this work among themselves, and friendly arguments often ensue. I write the Teeline on the board for them and we discuss any problems that may have arisen. Here, students begin to appreciate the flexibility of Teeline, for often there will be more than one way of writing the same word and they may choose whichever outline appeals or which suits their style of writing.

After a few weeks, the class will fall naturally into groups. There will probably be one group that will forge ahead, seeming to absorb everything with ease. These students often spend a lot of time working at home. Others may have difficulty and take much longer to assimilate the theory.

It is necessary to provide additional material for the more-able students, and this can be in the form of taped dictation passages. Many schools and colleges have a library of speed tapes as well as 'multi-listening' equipment, where a tape recorder can be plugged in and up to eight students equipped with head sets listen to the same tape. Of course, individual students can use a single tape recorder with a head set, if required.

Obviously, the lecturer's time must be equally divided between the students, so both sections of the class should spend some time working alone or with tapes while the teacher attends to the others. Try to make a point of speaking to students individually every week, giving help and encouragement where necessary and praise where it is due.

With Teeline, unseen dictation can be introduced in the early stages. Again, proceed from the known to the unknown. First dictate the words and sentences introduced in the lesson, getting the students to read back from their own notes. Then dictate sentences they have not seen before. Ask them to read what they have written, check and discuss the outlines, and then re-dictate two or three times, gradually increasing the speed.

Short, simple letters or other material can be introduced at an early stage. If unfamiliar words arise, write them on the board before the dictation starts, and get the students to read them aloud and copy them in their notebooks, so that when the word appears in the passage, it can be written without hesitation. Students may, at first, be reluctant to read aloud by themselves. If so, let them read in chorus. Later they can be asked to read according to the speed they have reached, the others helpfully calling out a missing word where necessary. Often this help is given rather too eagerly, giving the reader hardly time to pause for breath! There is often friendly competition to be the first to read back a difficult word or to achieve a higher speed.

Many students are diffident about taking examinations, particularly if they have been unsuccessful with other shorthand systems. However, without being too dogmatic about it, it is a good thing to encourage students to have a goal in view, and I would expect a student who attended regularly and completed the homework assignments to be ready to take an examination at 50 or 60 w.p.m. by the end of the session. As the students progress, I grade the dictation material accordingly, and introduce old examination papers as soon as they seem ready for them. Most examining bodies will supply old papers at very reasonable prices. The examinations organized by Teeline Education Ltd may be taken at any time provided at least 4 weeks' notice is given, and results come through within 4 weeks (see page viii). This is very useful, for one can distribute the certificates (which accompany the results) to the successful students, and this encourages the others to try.

For success, students should aim for a slightly higher speed than that required in the test. Most people are nervous when taking examinations, so having a little speed in hand can make the difference between success and failure. I usually arrange a mock test just before the examination, so that they will have some idea of what to expect at the actual examination.

In addition, ample practice in written transcription is essential, for this is quite different from reading aloud from one's notes. It is not really a good idea to spend valuable class time on this, however, but a transcript can be set for homework each week, and should be marked by the teacher. Students must be made aware of the importance of spelling and punctuation, as well as general presentation.

Sometimes friends may be able to meet during the week and take turns to dictate to each other. If, however, students have no one who is able or willing to dictate to them at home, then they can be advised to make use of the radio or television. I often suggest to students in the early stages of speed-building that they should try taking down the words of the songs played on *Top of the Pops*, or similar programmes, for there is usually plenty of repetition and the speed is well within their reach. If the school or college has a tape library, this solves many problems, but if not it is quite a simple matter to make tapes, or there are many sources from which they may be obtained. The main thing is to encourage students to use their Teeline as much as possible, even for such things as shopping lists.

With evening classes, problems of attendance and punctuality frequently arise. Many students will already have done a day's work, travelled home and then had to travel some distance to reach the class. Often, in bad weather, or if they are feeling tired or unwell, they may be tempted to stay away. If they stay away once or twice, it may be difficult for them to make the effort to come back. I have found it a good idea to send a postcard or short letter to absentees, saying that their absence has been noticed, that the class will be meeting as usual the following week, and that I hope to see them then. A student will often return when it is realized that you are sufficiently interested to write.

So far as punctuality is concerned, it is not a good idea to wait for late-comers to arrive. It is far better to start the class on time, irrespective of attendance, and students will soon make the effort to arrive punctually so that they will not miss anything. Some may ask to leave early in order to catch buses or trains, and while this is not to be encouraged, discretion must be used in cases where transport provision is poor.

I think, however, that Teeline generates so much interest among students that these problems are far less likely to arise than with other shorthand systems.

Chapter 15 Keeping Class Records

MURIEL O'DONNELL

In shorthand classes, regular progress tests should always be given. Not only do they show the teacher where there may be any weaknesses, but they are an indication to the student of the advance that has been made since the first lesson. Every teacher will have noticed the *frisson* of pleasure that goes through a class when told 'There you are – you have now written a passage at 40 words a minute. Who would have thought, two weeks ago, that you would be writing at 40 today?' The teacher might continue: 'Today, 40 may seem a very fast speed but next week, when you have advanced to 50, 40 will seem quite slow', and that is a challenge which they will gladly take up.

Before giving a test, it is necessary for teachers to recognize why they are testing and what they are testing. Essentially, shorthand and language are integrated. From the outset of learning, shorthand students must be made aware of the use and command of the language. Shorthand is not just a collection of rules and gimmicks. It is an art, a skill – the art of being able to take down dictation at high speeds and to transcribe the passage; and to re-present this in an acceptable form is a highly satisfactory and stimulating skill.

To achieve this, many aspects must be covered. Speed-building is obviously essential, but it would be pointless reaching a speed of, say 140 w.p.m., and finally producing work with poor spelling, or, worse still, not being able to read the shorthand and, therefore, not being able to transcribe it. So throughout the course, students must be made aware of their progress not only in speed, but in their aural comprehension, their reading ability and sentence structure, their use of grammar and spelling, and word usage and meaning. This can only be done if tests are made and records kept.

Class records serve four useful purposes:

1. They can indicate the progress of students and the ability of the tutor.
2. They can be an inducement to work. Most of us work and play better if there is an element of competition, but this element must be kept within limits and adjusted to the temperaments of students.
3. Tests can be used to help students to organize their knowledge and apply it during dictation.
4. At the end of the course, the day of reckoning may be expected. In shorthand it is the inevitable examination, at speed, with a good transcription.

There are other points the teacher will also consider, such as classwork and homework, attendance and the attitude of the student. Some tutors find such records useful in noting a particular point at which a student starts to slacken off.

In fact, testing and recording is taking place from the first lesson. Chalkboard reading, note reading, questions on theory and even watching the writing of students all serve the purpose of making the teacher aware of the progress and weaknesses of students. But none of this work is rated by a mark, so more formal tests must be introduced. The number and length of them will vary with the needs of the class, but some students respond better if frequent tests are done and others if testing is kept to a minimum. Therefore the frequency of them is something for the individual teacher to decide.

In daily classes, a weekly test is useful. Not only does this give students a realization of their progress; tests are a guide to the teacher of how the lessons are being absorbed. If several students show a weakness in any particular principle, then it may be that the teacher is at fault and it could well be worth considering a fresh approach so that in future the lesson is presented another way.

During the early stages, a test might be presented in two parts. First, twenty or thirty isolated words (including a sprinkling of special forms) which are dictated slowly; then a brief passage at a low speed within the capabilities of students, which they have to transcribe. Marks can be allocated out of 50 – one for each of the words and the remainder for 'speed', divided between the shorthand and the transcript.

If this is done during the last shorthand period on a Friday, the first lesson the following Monday can be devoted to pointing out faults and if necessary doing some revision. With evening classes, the teacher may decide to hold such a test every four weeks or so, but the same procedure can be followed.

Once the basic theory has been covered, the course should concentrate on three things:

1. To continue to build and broaden the knowledge – **general progress**.
2. To practise the skill over and over again, introducing more advanced techniques – **speed development**.
3. To transcribe this work within a given period of time – **transcription**.

Records should be kept from the beginning of the course, and there are several ways in which this can be done. Some teachers prefer an exercise book in which students' names are entered alphabetically; others make a card index for individual students; a third way is to have a large card or sheet of paper which provides an at-a-glance record for the entire class.

My own preference is for the latter, and it is arranged in the fashion shown in Table 15.1.

Date	Name	Theory	Shorthand style	Reading	Speed	Special forms	Word-groups

Table 15.1   General progress chart

From this chart I can see where each student's pitfalls lie and can then plan remedial work. In some cases individual attention is required, and in others a tape recording is useful in order to watch the writing process in action and, finally, in group dictation to encourage students to reach a speed goal.

Group tests must be administered in the proper way so that accurate information is obtained and the interpretation of those results acted upon. In the case of language difficulties the tutor in this subject should be consulted.

To encourage this general progress one must: 1. concentrate on the development of useful speeds; 2. insist on good posture; 3. maintain a balance between good outlines and speed; 4. avoid fatigue; 5. set attainable goals; 6. continually remind students how to increase their speed; 7. eliminate time-wasting movements; 8. encourage students to try to reach their targets.

When speed-building begins in earnest, different charts are used, but here again there are various methods of keeping records. Teachers with card indexes and exercise books will retain them throughout the course.

It should be remembered that a student cannot be considered capable of writing at a given speed on one transcript alone, and the class should be told this. It is the custom in many groups to permit a student to claim a certain speed when three passages have been taken and transcribed with 98 per cent accuracy. Quite often a student will 'get' a 60 and then take some time before doing so again, and the knowledge that *three* have to be done is a good incentive.

They will also become aware that whereas memory (immediate recall) plays a part in the transcription of low speeds, as the rate gets higher and the passages contain more words, greater reliance must be placed on the shorthand, since memory can be a fickle jade – witness the number of times a student gets behind at the end of dictation and as a result puts the words down in the wrong order, or forgets them completely.

One useful record the class can always refer to is the 'speed ladder' which is put on the wall. This is a card on which a ladder is drawn and each rung represents a speed which is clearly marked. Students' names are written on slips of card (or on cut-out figures if the teacher is of artistic bent) and fixed to the ladder by a drawing pin. These cards or figures are moved up rung by rung as the speed increases. One such ladder consisted of three rungs for each speed, and as each transcription was done satisfactorily the figure was moved up one rung. But beware of the joker who moves them up surreptitiously – the teacher must still keep a personal record.

My own speed chart is shown in Table 15.2.

	Sept.	Oct.	Nov.	Dec.	Jan.	Feb.	Mar.	Apr.	May	June
140										
130										
120										
110										
100										
90										
80										
70										
60										
50										
40										
30										

Table 15.2   Speed chart

To encourage speed development I have found it is best to:
1. demonstrate often; 2. preview work to be done and in some cases prepare for dictation; 3. check techniques constantly; 4. review techniques; 5. establish suitable standards; 6. remind students how to improve speed.

In addition to the speed chart, I also prefer to keep a record of transcription tests. Although no one can be said to write at a given speed until satisfactory transcriptions can be submitted, I have found it useful to analyse the work done. On TOPS courses it can be of help to students if their shortcomings in punctuation and spelling can be quietly pointed out to them individually, and in most cases they will make a conscious effort to overcome them.

In schools and colleges any faults that come to light in the transcripts can be referred to the tutor in English as well as to the student. The Teeline teacher should also deal with the subject in class if errors are not confined to one person. In this way the English lessons will be reinforced and as a shorthand student is judged by the transcript produced, this will also ensure an improvement.

Those teachers using the card index and book methods will of course maintain a transcription record, but I prefer a separate one, set out as in Table 15.3.

Date	Name	Inability to read shorthand	Slow transcript	Punctuation	Spelling	Poor general knowledge

Table 15.3   Transcription chart

The transcription chart applies only to handwritten transcripts, but it is easy to make provision for typing back by adding columns for speed and accuracy in typing. When a typewriter is used, the criteria should be: 1. material should be placed reasonably well, attractively and neatly laid out; 2. letters should follow the dictation closely; 3. there should be no errors of spelling, punctuation, capitalization or hyphenation; 4. there should be no uncorrected typographical errors and erasures should be made neatly; 5. there should be no omissions. In some schools, this assessment is done in collaboration with the teacher of typewriting.

Other tutors may have devised their own methods of keeping records which are different from those presented in this chapter. In evening classes, the teacher may wish to keep a very full record of students, including the home address, telephone number (home and office) and occupation, so that in the event of any absence a letter can be sent or a telephone call made. Where absence is the result of illness or bereavement, a note can be made in the records.

The method of assessment employed in keeping class records is essentially an individual matter. Every teacher has his or her way of marking. 'Correctness' of outline rarely enters into the assessment of Teeline, but at all times in the learning stage there should be a generous allocation of marks to pen control and neatness as well as to a judicious use of grouping and a knowledge of the special forms.

When examination time draws near and mock tests are given, these can be entered in ink of a different colour.

Examining bodies do not give details of their marking methods and the teacher should therefore set a high standard in assessment. In class work, some like to allow a margin of 5 per cent for error, but in mock tests 2 per cent is a more realistic figure. If records are to be of any benefit to the student – and they should be – then it might be best if the latter figure were adhered to throughout the course.

The point now remains: what is an error? It is known that some examining bodies differentiate between 'minor' errors and 'major' ones, but the teacher is not likely to know which is which and is therefore in no position to judge. Other bodies count subsequent repetitions of mistakes as being worth only the loss of half a mark.

So for class records, and to be on the safe side, the teacher should count each error as a penalty of one mark. Thus, in a two-minute passage at 100 w.p.m., the student fails if five or more errors are made, reckoning a pass mark at 98 per cent. This is a high standard but it will pay dividends, as class records of examination results by external bodies will soon show.

Chapter 16 Team Teaching

CELIA OSBORNE

Teeline is an ideal subject for team teaching, as its flexibility correlates readily with the necessary requirements for this system of tuition. There is no one method of team teaching and descriptions in this chapter are mainly applicable to Teeline. Other methods and concepts will be required for different types of schools or subjects.

Team teaching was first brought to notice about twenty years ago and has gradually gained support in many schools and colleges. Primarily, it is the formal co-operation between two or more teachers to plan and operate a teaching scheme for a group of students. A course is timetabled for a subject (or subjects) to make it possible for tutors to teach on a team basis. This involves careful 'scheme of work' planning so that the final product is a workable whole.

Historically, team teaching arose when the knowledge content of the curriculum increased beyond the capacity of individuals to contain a reasonable proportion of, and to be familiar with, the attendant theories.

It is of paramount importance that students understand the team-teaching concept, otherwise there is a danger that they will assume it to be a makeshift administrative arrangement for the convenience of the college. Explanation is particularly necessary if some classes are being taught in the conventional way, entirely by one tutor, and others by the team-teaching method.

The flexibility required from tutors helps to eliminate any individual authoritarian attitudes and this improves relationships between students and teachers. There is obviously a better chance of compatibility so far as the students are concerned if more than one tutor is involved. To experience a variety of teaching styles and different ways of learning can only be advantageous.

Tutors will need to change many of their own preconceived ideas in order to accommodate the opinions of others. In general, this will not be too difficult for commercial teachers, who might already have been employed as part of a team in the business world. They will gain from discovering new ideas and their perspective of the subject will widen during the necessary negotiations and planning sessions.

It is a sad reflection on the teaching profession that most practitioners work in a closed world of a single classroom. Team teaching shows them another world where they can become aware of the range of alternatives available by contact with other members of staff. This contact will show not only the successes but also the limitations of colleagues. Most importantly, tutors realize, by comparison, their own accomplishments and failures.

Those who are converting from other shorthand systems will be able to give their experience in speed-building and other aspects of shorthand theory to the less-experienced shorthand instructors and will themselves learn the more flexible approach required in the Teeline system.
Younger, weaker and student teachers are helped to develop and improve by working with experienced tutors.

No one can hope to be expert in, or even interested in, all aspects of the subject or of the teaching role. We all have our preferences for different parts of theory or stages of teaching as, for example, a higher proficiency at reading some speeds than others. These preferences and proficiencies are conveyed to students by our enthusiasm or the lack of it, and it is important that planning sessions should include opportunities for tutors to express preferences for particular aspects of teaching. In this way instruction abilities are maximized for the benefit of students.

Part-time tutors will gain from team teaching by closer integration with other members of staff and discussion between colleagues. Their knowledge of college facilities and the availability of resources will be improved, and they may well be able to make a contribution by their more recent contact with secretarial and commercial practices in the business field.

Marking, keeping registers, records of students' work and timetabling can be shared, thus lessening the administrative load. These registers and record books could be located in one room, which could also contain other resources and material required for the group.

One member of the group should be given responsibility for the organization of the resources room. This may be a tutors' room or merely a storage cupboard, depending upon circumstances.

If conditions permit a room, this could also be the meeting place for planning, decisions and the exchange of information. Once the team is working well, coffee or lunch breaks are quite adequate for discussion once a week and this will not then become a 'meeting' chore. These discussions should be informal and congenially conducted.

To give a class viewpoint, a student representative may in some situations be included occasionally at the planning meetings. This would help to ensure the necessary confidence and understanding of the students. As a by-product, the students would learn the need for organization within groups and the role of the secretary at meetings, i.e. a useful transfer of learning aspect.

In addition to student registers and record books, the group room or cupboard could also contain timetables, tapes, dictation material, overhead projector sheets, speed passages and a notebook for special messages.

From the college point of view, team teaching provides an efficient use of staff. A small business studies department in a college, or a small college, can make far better use of full-time staff augmented by part-timers by using this method. Some private commercial colleges employ solely part-time staff by using team teaching, thus using staff only when required. It allows for more flexible timetabling and enables any member of the team to take over in cases of absence from another member of the staff at short notice.

Furthermore, the preparation of teaching aids is minimized. Tutors can each prepare a few cassette tapes at varying dictation speeds, and these can be copied for use by all tutors or for use at home by students. A cassette copier is an essential piece of equipment in shorthand classes.

Individual tutors can contribute dictation passages and exercises for copying and general use. Such common-sense practices lessen the workload as a whole and allow a more effective use of resources.

The composition of the team is most important. There will be members of staff who cannot coexist agreeably or do not want to work within a group. To include such a person will bring inevitable failure. Tact by the head of the department or co-ordinator will be required in setting up a group. It needs to be well prepared and patience is necessary until the possible rigidity of some members of the teaching staff is relaxed and they become amenable to the idea of team teaching.

At first, interpersonal discords may arise and these will require diplomacy by the co-ordinator of the group. All members of the team must understand what they are expected to do and must agree to integrate their activities and resources. Flexibility and compatibility of staff must be the paramount aim.

A course tutor can be put in charge to hold the group together at the beginning and be responsible for pooling resources and concepts; later, as staff become familiar with the idea, responsibilities can be interchanged. The co-ordinator will probably like to sit in at weekly discussion sessions occasionally to review progress until the group is working together as a whole.

Co-ordinating meetings could normally be held on an *ad hoc* basis as required, but it may be necessary to timetable some meetings on a more formal basis in order to deal with such items as initial preparation, planning ahead and changes of approach as the term progresses. It may also become necessary to adjust arrangements to accommodate the needs of individual students.

The problem of students playing-off one member of the team against another can normally be easily overcome by good organization of team and flexibility of teachers if and when such a situation arises. Students must, however, understand that although tutors have different views and standards, objectives are the same, and students themselves should acquire flexibility in dealing with problems. All tutors should be able to follow the same syllabus in their own way. The flexibility of the Teeline system is applicable here.

There is no one way of organizing team teaching. It is a new concept and must change from class to class. Each team will be different and develop along its own lines, depending upon the type of college, students, instructors and facilities available.

In subjects such as history, geography or languages, the team-teaching format commences with a lead or key lesson with several classes combined to provide the students with initial interest and stimulus. This key lesson is given further impetus by combined follow-up work taking place within conventional classes or in an interest-centred group, where students in several classes are working to form a whole project. It is a method of dealing with mixed-ability groups, using the talents and aptitudes of students whether academic, practical or imaginative.

This situation would be difficult to deal with in the business studies field, where shorthand and typewriting, at least, are progressive skills. Office practice, business studies or secretarial studies would probably be ideal subjects for team teaching using the respective talents of all students, and would enliven interest in the subject, each tutor giving the benefit of their knowledge and experience of, strengths in and enthusiasms for, its different aspects.

If circumstances allowed, team teaching covering Teeline, typewriting and office practice etc. could, if well organized, make an interesting course.

Accommodation is necessarily stereotyped in business studies courses – rooms are completely occupied by typewriters which are generally timetabled to be in use at all times. This militates against the idea of flexibility. Nevertheless, a Teeline class or classes can be held together very well with team teaching. The combined classes come at the end of the course with speed-building sessions. This is the reverse of the more usual concept of team teaching.

As the team will involve several lecturers using their own ideas, a variety of voices and styles of dictation will give students some experience which can be applied to the work situation. The ever-present problem of satisfying all students in a speed class can more easily be solved by using the team-teaching method. It is simple to divide classes into various speed groups, or for remedial instruction. Students are able to move from one group to another as they themselves decide on their individual needs.

Contrary to the debatable streaming in other subjects, shorthand students are usually only too pleased to be moved into speed groupings. Their general complaint, in a single tutor class, is that they are not getting enough dictation in their personal speed range. Given time to work at their individual pace gives confidence, which in turn improves attitudes and motivation.

Team planning rather than team teaching may be the end result, but the idea is still a useful one to bring various perspectives to light and to create a dialogue between Teeline tutors having different methods of teaching, thus learning from each other. Team teaching is comparable to an orchestra where musicians play their own instruments from individual scores in order to present the complete work. This is not unlike tutors following their own lesson plans as part of a scheme of work within the syllabus.

Team teaching is difficult to define specifically because it can take so many different forms. In summary, however, one may state that team teaching is an organizational concept rather than a new teaching technique, and is concerned with the organization of the areas to be studied, how the goal/objectives are to be achieved, and the policies adopted for the assessment of attainment.

In more precise terms, it may be described as a form of organization in which individual instructors decide to pool resources, interests and expertise in order to devise and implement a scheme of work suitable to the needs of their pupils and the facilities of their college.

Some areas of integration could be: *Humanities*: English, history, geography, religious education; *Crafts*: woodwork, metalwork, needlework, home economics; *Sciences*: biology, physics, chemistry, mathematics; *Business Studies*: office practice, Teeline, typewriting.

The tutors in these areas, by actively co-operating and pooling their resources (i.e. specialization, interests, skills, knowledge, experience and personality), decide how best these can be used to serve the needs of the students.

The advantages and disadvantages may be summarized as follows:

Advantages: greater variety – increases interest; avoids duplication of subject areas; more effective use of tutor; more efficient use of resources; pooling of knowledge.

Disadvantages: more difficult to administer; requires staff compatibility; more demanding of tutor; student adjustment required.

Further reading

D. Warwick, *Team Teaching* (University of London Press, 1971).
L. Curzon, *Teaching in Further Education* (Cassell, 1976).
A. Adams, *Team Teaching and the Teaching of English* (Pergamon, 1970).

Chapter 17 An Examiner's View

GEORGE HILL

Far more candidates pass than fail their Teeline examinations. This is clearly unfair. Tongue firmly in cheek, I shall try to redress the balance by offering some advice to those who would like to fail but find it difficult, presumably because Teeline is so easy.

1. Make sure you sit the exam at a speed you cannot do.
2. Work yourself up into a highly nervous state before the examination commences. This will ensure that your writing hand will either be stricken with rigor mortis or produce grotesque outlines which could be deciphered only by an eminent cryptologist.
3. Do not concentrate on the passage being dictated. Think about your dog or your girl- or boyfriend.
4. Write H through the line and P on the line at the beginning of an outline. Deal similarly with D and T.
5. Use a blunt pencil or a blobby pen and check that there is no other writing implement at hand which you might be tempted to use if your pencil breaks or your pen dries up.
6. Scatter a few longhand words among your Teeline outlines. You will lose at least one mark for each of these.
7. If you are submitting a handwritten transcript, make sure it is largely illegible.
8. Do not try to punctuate either your notes or transcript. Alternatively, punctuate at random without giving any thought to the sense of the passage.
9. While transcribing, alter and generally mess up your Teeline outlines. This will make the examiner suspicious – and you will not get the benefit of any doubt.
10. Have something to eat or drink during the test. There is nothing more likely to annoy the examiner than finding a few breadcrumbs embedded in a tea-stained transcript.

Tongue now removed from cheek, let us have a close look at the mistakes that appear repeatedly in either notes or transcripts. As might be expected, pride of place goes to the carelessly written outline. Confusion between short, common words is the most frequent reason for lost marks and, precisely because they are common words, one of the most frequent causes of failure.

Teachers would do a great service to their students if, at an early stage, they would ensure that all the words in the following list can be written unambiguously. The words are grouped to show the most

96

common mistranscriptions. Note that some words appear in more than one group:

on/with/your   I/you/we   as/is/us   this/these/those   in/an/on   any/only
at/to   if/for   while/where   what/out   of/very/you   I/it   can/could
shall/should   of/to   the/top   why/where   from/for

It is especially important to write an unmistakable outline for the word *I*. More marks are lost through misreading *I* for *it* or *you* than through any other single error, although confusion between *we* and *you* comes a close second. In these cases, context is not a reliable guide. Many years ago, I decided to eliminate the *I/it/you* problem by teaching the use of the indicator instead of the full vowel for the word *I*, and to reduce the *we/you* problem by 'drilling in' the correct outlines as soon as they had been demonstrated to my students. My experience as an examiner proves I was right to do so.

Before going any further, there are several important points that must be made. First, by concentrating on errors I may be giving the impression that there are many more of these than is, in fact, the case. Secondly, they are made principally by inexperienced Teeliners, often very young and not highly educated, who are attempting their first shorthand examinations at 50 or 60 w.p.m. Indeed, before Teeline came along many of them would have been denied the chance to learn the skill of fast-writing on the grounds of low educational attainment and, in particular, a poor standard of English. Thirdly, examinations are failed for many different reasons, some of which are unconnected with badly written outlines.

Here is another cautionary list in which pairs or groups of words are sometimes confused for one or more of these reasons: badly written outlines; careless positioning; ignorance of the meaning of a word; misuse of a Teeline principle; neglect of a Teeline principle; failure to understand or think about context; failure to make use of a distinguishing outline:

alternate/alternative   act/decide   decision/discussion
account/income   city/county/country/century   case/cause
committee/community   detail/total   appear/appeal   effect/affect
eatable/edible   equally/today   her/high   find/found   here/higher
granted/guaranteed   made/met   female/family   gardens/grounds
January/June   lovely/lively   best/last/least   post/position
prices/prizes   had/put/paid   send/signed/sound   perhaps/propose
small/smaller/similar   written/routine   personal/personnel
prosecute/persecute   stable/suitable   station/situation   good/great
debt/debit   fact/factor   different/difficult   gradually/greatly
special/social/school   minute/moment/month   whether/other
read/write/reader/writer   arrangement/argument   argued/agreed
Miss/Mrs

Obvious spelling mistakes carry no penalty, but homonyms do present a problem. Transcriptions such as *we walked passed the building sight* and *it is quite common for people to loose there way* make me wonder if the candidate had any real understanding of the passage. Other 'spelling mistakes' of this type are: *threw/through know/no knew/new steal/steel here/hear where/wear blew/blue.*

No one, I suppose, knows the meaning of every single word in the English language, but shorthand teachers usually possess a wider vocabulary than their students and it is part and parcel of their job to make sure that every word they dictate is understood by every student. After all, enlarging one's vocabulary is an essential part of speed-building.

It may be unfortunate for some candidates, but examination passages are not written to a strictly limited vocabulary. I see quite a few examples of candidates who manage to get down an outline – often a correct one – for an unfamiliar word but are then unable to transcribe it. Sometimes they make amusing or amazing guesses. Consider the word *trousseau.* According to recent transcripts we should not be concerned about the cost of the bride's trousseau, but about the cost of her tears, trews, torso, truss or drawers!

Some candidates are quite crafty. Uncertain of the meaning of a particular outline, they offer two different words in the transcript. All to no avail. Far from saving at least half a mark, they will probably lose a whole one. A similar ploy is to coin a brand-new word from two old ones. I was impressed by *instroduction* (an instructional introduction?) and *alcolollic* (an inebriating lolly?) but, alas, they were not the words dictated.

All too often I have the sad duty of failing a candidate who submits a complete Teeline note with a transcript which, through sheer carelessness, is incomplete. Sometimes an entire line of the note has been overlooked; sometimes a complete sentence has been ignored. Not infrequently, the salutations at the end of a letter are not transcribed. I am sure such errors of omission are often the result of inadequate training in the art of transcription. The time allowed for transcription is not ungenerous and candidates should make full use of it. I wonder how much thought, how much checking and rechecking, went into the production of this transcript: *We are sure you will agree that this is an offer you really cannot afford.* Nothing at all wrong with it – as far as it goes. However, the sentence came towards the end of a letter praising the virtues of that particular offer and it clearly makes no sense in that context. Moreover, the candidate omitted the words *to turn down* from the end of the sentence although the outlines were in her note.

The lack of punctuation, especially in the Teeline note, is yet another familiar problem. Teachers must take a large share of the blame for this. Full stops omitted from the note make transcribing a hazardous task

because it is not always obvious where they should be put. To drive
home this important point, here is an extreme example of an incorrectly
punctuated passage – not part of a test piece, I assure you! *Out comes the
film star on her head. She wears a magnificent tiara on her fingers.
Diamonds sparkle as she opens her mouth to speak to the photographers. A
warm breeze gently lifts her silvery skirt high above her head. The circling
doves* . . . . Marks are lost in an examination if the transcript is
punctuated in a way that causes a change in the sense or meaning of the
passage.

And so we come to the biggest single cause of failure. Why so many
students are made to sit the test at a speed they cannot possibly manage
is quite beyond my comprehension. This practice is particularly
widespread at the lower speeds. Teachers should ask themselves what is
the effect on students who take their first shorthand examination without
the remotest chance of success. What future confidence are those
students going to have in Teeline as a shorthand system? What
confidence in the teacher? What confidence in their own ability?

In many ways those first examinations are the most important of all,
yet the pass rate at 50 w.p.m. is the lowest of all at about 60 per cent. If
eight out of every ten candidates can pass at 70 w.p.m., the same number
at 90, and seven out of every ten at 120, there is no acceptable reason for
a failure rate of around 40 per cent at 50 w.p.m.

Incidentally, 'nerves' is often the excuse put forward by the
unsuccessful candidate, but which of these two candidates would be the
more nervous: a 100 writer attempting 90 or a 40 writer attempting 50?
I know that teachers do not always have the final word about who is
going to attempt which speed, but to condemn someone to certain failure
in a speed test is nothing less than mental cruelty and teachers who
condone it are guilty of dereliction of professional duty.

I find it puzzling that so few candidates make use of the methods that
have been suggested in Teeline textbooks for recording large round
numbers. Are those methods not being taught? If not, why not? Many
candidates pay a stiff penalty for trying to record *million* or *hundred
thousand* as a succession of noughts. Some do not seem to know the
correct number of noughts and others get it wrong, anyway. Some get it
right, but only at the expense of missing the next few words. Simply
writing the full Teeline outlines for *hundred, thousand, million* etc. would
be better than strings of noughts, but few candidates do even that.

Too many teachers are teaching too much theory before starting their
students on the speed-building ladder. The synthesis of what used to be
called 'basic' Teeline and 'advanced' Teeline seems to have given
teachers the impression that all published Teeline theory (with the
unfortunate exception of numbers) should be taught before students
attempt their first test at 50 w.p.m. Unhappily, this can be achieved only
if the theory-learning stage is considerably lengthened or valuable

practice time is sacrificed. As an examiner, I see the results of this in notes containing half-learnt and badly applied 'advanced' principles cheek by jowl with equally unsatisfactory attempts at applying such elementary principles as the omission of unnecessary letters or the simple joining of letters. It is no wonder such candidates are unable to transcribe their notes accurately.

In contrast, I recently marked a small set of scripts from a comprehensive school: not a PL blend to be seen; 'large D' used at the start of a word; hardly a blend to be found; even common word endings like -ABLE and -MENT completely ignored, and no two words joined together! In short, it was quite the most primitive Teeline I had seen in many a long year. But how effective! Almost every candidate passed, several with distinction, at 80 and 90 w.p.m. It certainly could not have taken them very long to learn so little theory. They should now be ready for a bit more theory to help them surge past 'the 100'.

It is high time I paid my compliments to the thousands of excellent Teeline writers – and scores of conscientious teachers – whose labours make my intrinsically tedious task worthwhile. Despite rumours to the contrary, examiners are human. As such, we prefer the beautiful to the ugly, the tidy to the untidy, the clean to the dirty. I enjoy marking attractive transcripts. If they look good, they usually are good. In any case, I feel well disposed towards these candidates and, if they turn out to be borderline cases, they will get the benefit of the doubt.

I would like to see more typed transcripts, which can be marked more quickly, but I do get a lot of handwritten ones which are nicely set out and can be easily read without the aid of a microscope. I also see many excellent Teeline notes. However, I do wish that all teachers would instruct candidates not to tamper with their original notes when transcribing. Seeing alterations to the outlines makes me suspect that some kind of cheating may have taken place and there is no benefit of any doubt in such cases!

Finally, a few of my favourite mistranscriptions. Some of them verge on the hilarious, but they also serve as examples of the points I have made about spelling, lack of thought when transcribing, inaccurate positioning, poor vocabulary and so on.

1. ... here is your mortgage *production* policy ...
2. ... I look forward to the *pressure* of seeing you ...
3. ... on the *scarface* we have a good record ...
4. ... we will be better off in the long *trim* ...
5. ... we may have to *feed* the bill for repairs ...
6. ... we provide *metal* test papers and answers ...
7. ... your *corporation* will be appreciated ...
8. ... by taking out an *endearment* policy ...
9. ... such bad habits as smoking and *tracking dogs* ...

10. . . . beating about the *brush* . . .
11. . . . the cost of *roar* materials . . .
12. . . . a little *stockholing* in the previous year . . .
13. . . . an extra *runaway* at the airport . . .
14. . . . I *computed* between my home and London . . .
15. . . . land which has been *airmarked* for . . .
16. . . . this is an area where *economics* could be made . . .
17. . . . members of the *pubic* are welcome . . .
18. . . . cannot balance the family *budgie* . . .
19. . . . braille helps blind *magicians* to read music . . .
20. . . . *diary* products like cheese and butter . . .
21. . . . the girls are involved in a *sandal* . . .
22. . . . I hope you will not be too *embraced* . . .
23. . . . will help to keep wood from *rooting* . . .
24. . . . average *yearnings* have risen . . .
25. . . . materials such as *creep* . . .
26. . . . three possible *curses* of action . . .
27. . . . a help to *tedious* housewives . . .
28. . . . seventy per cent of all *germs* are made by *cures* . . .

Just in case you were baffled by any of these howlers, here is a checklist: 1. protection 2. pleasure 3. surface 4. term 5. foot 6. model 7. co-operation 8. endowment 9. taking drugs 10. bush 11. raw 12. stockpiling 13. runway 14. commuted 15. earmarked 16. economies 17. public 18. budget 19. musicians 20. dairy 21. scandal 22. embarrassed 23. rotting 24. earnings 25. crepe 26. courses 27. today's 28. journeys, cars.

Chapter 18 Teeline in the Technological Age

DOROTHY FORD

Microelectronics have had a greater impact on world communications than any other invention since the wheel. Information Technology Year 1982 marked the effect the silicon chip is having in bringing about the automation of office procedures. It has brought about a dramatic reduction in capital costs with circuits costing thousands of pounds in the 1940s being produced for a few pence, and has enabled a vast range of machines to be automated which are compact, reliable and have a low power consumption.

Several inventions over the last hundred years have been of significance to the office – the telephone, the typewriter, the audio-machine, the photocopier, the computer. They have all contributed in some way to simplifying and speeding up existing office procedures rather than bringing about any fundamental change.

One of the great changes occurred in 1873 when the first typing machine was commercially produced and girls began to be employed as 'typewriters'. Even so, women did not start to take over in offices until the First World War. Shorthand was given a great boost at this time, and today there are more shorthand writers than before.

Dictation-machine manufacturers have, however, been sounding the death-knell for shorthand ever since the first dictating machine was launched following the invention of the telephone in 1876. But shorthand still lives, and while people continue to make speeches, such utterances will require to be recorded and reproduced so there will be a demand for the shorthand writer and the journalist.

The manufacturers of audio equipment saw their machines as the employers' answer to the problems of the inaccuracies of shorthand-typists. In the event, shorthand-typists were able to add another skill to their accomplishments, and copy-typists to develop their talents and hold down more interesting and varied jobs.

However, many of these highly trained, efficient audio-typists found their output diminished because the executives could not use the system effectively. If improvements in productivity brought about by the new technology are to be maintained and inflation thereby offset, then poor executive performance must not be tolerated.

Executives need to be adequately trained in all aspects of the new technology if they are to install the right system for their particular business and be capable of communicating their wishes correctly. Sales representatives are always eager to push their products, making claims that cannot always be justified, and executives need to be fully aware of the type of hardware, back-up and software that will suit their own requirements before embarking on fundamental changes in procedures.

In spite of the recent developments in word processors, there will be for many years yet the orthodox office where the expense and reorganization involved in 'going electronic' cannot be justified.

In the electronic office it is the routine jobs – those of the copy-typist and junior shorthand-typist – that are at risk: their work can be more efficiently produced by means of the word processor with its *skilled* operator. There will be no room for the mediocre typist. However, note-taking, a shorthand skill, will still be required at higher levels of management because employers will want their personal assistants or personal secretaries to be capable of dealing with correspondence, reports, and a variety of other work from brief dictated instructions, ending the necessity for full, time-consuming dictation. This brings with it the need for competence in other sub-skills – that of composing from brief notes, which entails a sound knowledge of grammar, sentence structure, semantics, spelling, punctuation and so on.

Employers still ask for high speeds in the separate skills of shorthand and typewriting when advertising for a secretary/personal assistant. In some cases this is done because employers see such qualifications as a guide to the applicant's mental agility and ability to cope under stress; in others it is stated that high speeds are important so that correspondence, etc. can be dealt with quickly in order to release the secretary for more important administrative work. The post becomes that of an administrative assistant, one who is not tied to the typewriter but who has the necessary skills to deal with the routine work speedily and efficiently and also to delegate.

The speed of technological development must bring about fundamental changes in the secretarial training field so that courses are geared to present-day requirements within industry and commerce, and not tied to the limitations of timetables and availability/capabilities of the staff, so that students are suitably equipped to cope with working in the electronic office as well as the orthodox office. Reports in recent years by the Royal Society of Arts (*Office Technology: the implications for education and training in the 1980s*, June 1981) and the Manpower Services Commission (*Clerical and Commercial Training in the 1980s* and *The Way Forward*, both March 1981), point to the need for basic changes in the balance of subjects within the curriculum.

Emphasis should be on communication skills, background to business, office practice and keyboarding, an appreciation of and familiarity with the principles of word processing and some 'hands-on' experience. In addition to these basic subjects the RSA recommend specialist options to be provided in accounting, audio-typewriting, data preparation and handling, languages, law, office machinery and systems, quantitative methods in business, secretarial duties, and some form of shorthand/ note-taking. Thus there must be a reduction in the time allocated to shorthand training, and schools and colleges must look for systems that require less hours of instruction but which still have the potential for development to a high level of proficiency, reliability and credibility.

In the past as much as 50 per cent of the office studies curriculum has been devoted to achieving competence in shorthand and typewriting, and an excessive number of hours have been wasted in trying to teach shorthand to students who should never have been allowed to enter the shorthand classroom because of their lack of grounding in English language. Today's requirements would appear to demand speeds of around 100 w.p.m., and if such a standard can be reached in 100 hours or less, as it can with Teeline, then that is the system to be adopted.

Progress is always dependent upon the student's ability with language, its construction, semantics, etc. Without this facility, speedy and accurate transcription becomes impossible. Employers should be more concerned with the transcription rate than with the separate shorthand and typewriting speeds, and their insistence on such realistic qualifications would ensure that students took examinations appropriate to developing this transcription skill. Thus, the means by which the 'end product' is arrived at becomes less important.

Shorthand teachers must look to the future, not only for themselves but for their students; they should be teachers of shorthand, not teachers of one particular system of shorthand or note-taking. They should be the people who decide on the system to be adopted which best suits students' career expectations in the light of current developments, and be able to make the correct decision quite dispassionately.

Teachers must not allow themselves to be labelled 'die-hard' or 'stick-in-the-mud'; they must be forward-looking and be in a position to advise students as a result of their own working knowledge of the systems that are available. Every office skills teacher must be flexible, having already been 'liberalized', in order to be considered employable in the modern secretarial studies department.

Teeline is of the age of microtechnology: it evolved from the inventor's experience of teaching shorthand over a long period of time. He called it 'work study applied to longhand' and claimed, quite rightly, that any person capable of writing longhand is capable of writing Teeline. It is a flexible system. It can be taught as an exact science or, at the other extreme, as a means of making notes for one's own personal use.

In my experience it has been taught successfully since its invention to journalists. It has also been taught to students who have qualified for the Medical Secretary's Diploma, the LCCI Private Secretary's Certificate and Diploma, the RSA Diploma for Personal Assistants and the Bi-Lingual Secretary's Diploma. At the other end of the scale it has been taught to physically handicapped and educationally retarded students who have had a new interest, a new dimension, added to their lives – it increases their ability to communicate.

Teachers should learn the system and make themselves aware of the potentialities of Teeline – how the learning load is lightened, the necessity for so much homework eliminated, the time spent drilling substantially reduced, the stresses eliminated. Teeline is self-motivating. After the alphabet has been introduced (and being based on the already familiar letters this is quickly assimilated) the whole of the English language becomes available for use as dictation material.

Because of its low learning load it becomes a usable skill much more quickly, a tool of industry and commerce, and therefore motivation does not waver, but is in fact stimulated by its rapid usability and reliability.

In this day and age when speed of achievement is the criterion that recommends a skill, whether it be note-taking or driving a racing car, it is the speed of acceleration that is the deciding factor. With Teeline this speed of acceleration can be worked at almost immediately. It can be applied so realistically at such an early stage that any subject can be tackled so long as there is a pronounceable word for it. One can just as easily take notes about the mighty microchip as one can take notes about the lowly chip that goes with fish. A limited vocabulary puts the brakes on learning; therefore a note-taking system that covers the whole range of a language so quickly is one that is bound to appeal in this technological age.

The office has always been the centre of a communications network. It is the machinery used to process and communicate such information that has changed so fundamentally, and it behoves all employers and educationalists to keep abreast of such changes and their effect on the training of workers, existing as well as prospective. Prejudice and conservatism must not be allowed to overrule commonsense and therefore hinder progress.

This ability to communicate requires a broad basic education, with special attention being paid to literacy and numeracy, not only at secondary level and beyond but in the primary and junior schools, where technological aids can be used to assist in their development. With the consequent improvement in literacy there should be an improvement in the skill of using words and a consequent interest in reading and writing for its own sake.

This will all lead to improved proof-reading skills through a better knowledge of words, their meaning and spelling. Keyboard training also helps to improve linguistic ability. All this should lead to such an interest in the use of words that students will be more willing to listen to speakers and should be encouraged to learn a note-taking system that will enable them to record the spoken word.

Note-taking has been a necessary tool since the beginning of civilization, from the cuneiform characters of 2400 BC which were probably formed at about 20 w.p.m. through to present-day high-speed shorthand writers. Until such time as 'voice-on' replaces 'hands-on', which would necessitate a machine capable of replacing the human brain and ear with its powers of discrimination, there will always be a call for the shorthand writer in law courts, parliaments and assemblies of all kinds.

In the business world and in secretarial studies, time is the enemy – shorthand must and will have to take a back seat in time allocation in the secretarial curriculum, and if only 2–3 hours a week can be spared then Teeline is the answer. The cost-effectiveness of a system such as Teeline, the theory of which can be covered in 24 hours, is clear.

All staff must be prepared for change and be willing to add to their present skills and knowledge whether in industry or in education. In-service training should be available to enable staff to bring themselves up to date, and teacher-training courses should be so structured that new entrants to the profession are fully capable of teaching the new skills required.

No longer should skills be taught by untrained teachers: this practice has diluted the profession for far too long. Students should now be channelled into courses where their basic abilities can best be developed. There is no room for wastage: their keyboarding skills must be accurate to be of use in a word-processing unit: their note-taking/audio/transcription rate must be reliable and realistic.

Examination requirements need to be reviewed. The emphasis has to be placed on a student's ability to solve problems, and less emphasis placed on the finer points of the manual skills. The needs of the wide-ranging aspects of the technical and business world must be recognized and met and students must likewise be adequately trained to equip them as workers in the office of the future. Students must have access to electric typewriters, text-editing machines, electronic typewriters and the like if not actual operational instruction.

As far back as 1964 IBM invented a magnetic tape typewriter which had a memory, and the subsequent corrected text could be automatically typed at around 180 w.p.m. Today's operators will need to be fast, accurate typists, with the ability to remain seated for long periods of time – the equipment is far too expensive to be allowed to remain idle. An operator will need to be an efficient proof-reader, have good language skills and good transcription ability from longhand or audio, and have a logical mind to enable problems of layout, etc. to be solved. Audio-typewriting training will be of paramount importance. The word processor incorporates devices that enable checks to be made on the number of keystrokes made by each operator, so the ability to work under such stresses must be inculcated, as will the ability to concentrate in high ambient noise levels.

There is a need for an awareness of the possible convergence of equipment within the electronic office – the linking of the photocopier to the telephone to provide a facsimile transmission capability, to the word processor and to the personal computer. One or more of these machines might be combined in a single unit to fit on the desk top.

Facsimile transmission takes us into the realm of electronic mail, whereby the viewdata terminals will lead to the paperless business world, bringing about enormous savings in several areas, but creating many more redundancies. Further advances of significance to the office are bound to arrive in the form of voice-activated keyboards ('speaking machines'), but these are only just on the horizon and conventional keyboards will be needed for a long time.

Equally the conventional office will be with us for some time to come, and with it the need for the shorthand writer. The computer has to be programmed to 'think'. Human beings alone are capable of original thought and while this situation prevails, a note-taking system will be necessary to capture those original thoughts accurately and to record them for posterity. In these technological times, Teeline is the system.

PART TWO

Chapter 19 Preparing for the RSA Teachers' Diploma in Shorthand

MERIEL BOWERS

The syllabus for the RSA Teachers' Diploma in Shorthand stipulates every candidate must attend an approved course of instruction. Part Two of this book supplements such a course by giving a brief indication to the would-be teacher of what to expect before embarking on it. It is presented in simple terms that will be easily understood by the learner with no previous knowledge of teaching principles, but is not intended to be comprehensive nor to cut across what might be taught on the course. It is, in effect, a taster to whet the appetite for the many excellent reference books on educational psychology, principles and method which should then be read carefully. One might be prompted to think 'What has the child in the junior school' or 'What have the milestones in an under five's life as described by Gesell in his norms' to do with me as a would-be teacher of shorthand? The answer is that a knowledge of psychology is absolutely vital before we can begin to understand what makes the student 'tick'.

The course leading to an initial certificate is of two years' duration and contains a compulsory component of at least 10 hours' teaching practice. The syllabus comprises two parts – Part I: Theory and Application of Teeline Shorthand, consisting of two compulsory sections, and Part II: Principles and Methods of Learning and Teaching.

Examination structure

Part I: 2 hours' written exam set and marked by the RSA, normally taken at the end of the first year. This includes a dictated passage at 60 w.p.m. and two printed passages of 100 words, with a typed transcription.

Part II: Three components – (a) course work – teaching practice, assessed by course tutor; (b) course work – assignments, devised and assessed by the course tutor, within the Board's guidelines; (c) written exam – at the end of the second year. This is a paper of 3 hours' duration, set and marked by the Board.

Full details about entry requirements and the examination can be obtained in a booklet available from the Royal Society of Arts.

Although the RSA syllabus is set out in two parts, they should not be dealt with in isolation but instead must be integrated. Thus the student should understand the underlying educational principles in the construction of a lesson plan with the rules for skill-building also observed. Even though the Part I examination is normally taken at the end of the first year, it must not be assumed that Year I is simply based on practical shorthand work: the relevant parts of the Year II syllabus must be included to enable lesson plans to be made, employing the appropriate teaching methods when undergoing classroom experience early on in the course.

As Teeline is such an easy system to learn, with very little revision necessary for someone who has the basic entry qualifications for the examination, this ensures an excellent opportunity for integrating the various parts without a heavy revisionary load. The beauty of the system is its simplicity, and it is difficult to see at the time of writing how the theory can be extended to fill up most of the first year of the course. It cannot be too strongly emphasized, however, that candidates' knowledge of the system must be up to date and in accordance with current Teeline practice as indicated in *Teeline Revised Edition* and *Teeline Shorthand Made Simple*.

Assignments

An integral part of the examination is that a number of assignments (nine) have to be completed at varying intervals throughout the course. They are devised, set and marked by the course tutor on a 5-point scale ranging from A–E and they cover all nine sections of the syllabus (*q.v.*). Some of the assignments will be worked at home, some in class, and they may be either 'short' (perhaps taking the form of a short essay or multipart questions) or 'long'. One of the latter assignments will probably be given during the summer vacation between the two years of the course and may consist of several parts.

Preparing a syllabus and scheme of work

The RSA syllabus expects candidates to be able to construct business-like syllabuses, schemes of work and lesson plans, but candidates are often unsure of themselves when faced with the task of preparing these. They should be attempted at a very early stage in the course, otherwise teaching practice and classroom experience cannot be undertaken. Teaching practice is a learning situation for candidates so it cannot be too highly stressed how important it is to have properly prepared material, not least as a morale booster before entering the classroom.

A syllabus

This is a model of the subject-matter to be dealt with in a term, a session, or a course. Nowadays, it is often set out in objectival form with decimal enumeration to show the sub-divisions, although there is no particular order of presentation. It may be given to the teacher by an examining body, the course tutor, or in certain circumstances it may be necessary to draw up one's own.

Scheme of work

The syllabus must be organized into a scheme of work. This sets out the matter to be covered into an ordered sequence progressing logically from one topic to the next. In subjects such as commerce or office practice the topics that are easiest to learn are generally taught first; however, with a shorthand beginners' group, one starts from the complete unknown and the scheme of work must then follow the pattern of the textbook to be used. The scheme can be broken down into either a week-by-week or lesson-by-lesson structure but the anticipated student attainment at the end of the term/session/course depends upon:

(a) the number of available teaching hours;
(b) the number of hours the class meets each week;
(c) the type of class – high or low ability, day release, evening student, link course, etc.

Allowance must be made in the scheme of work for revision which should follow a cyclic plan. The material to be included should be challenging and there must be correlation with other subjects – typewriting, English and transcription. Full-time students will automatically have more practice material included because they spend more hours in the classroom. Care should be taken that practice passages are not included for theory not yet covered.

A scheme of work must be flexible. Bad weather, minor epidemics, fire drills and public transport strikes can quickly cast aside the best laid schemes, so it might not be possible to adhere to it rigidly; nevertheless, it provides a necessary framework.

A typical scheme of work might look like this:

Scheme of work

Class: full-time secretarial, Year I *Time:* 1 hour daily, 5 days a week
Age: 16+ *Textbook: Teeline Revised Edition*
3 CSEs: Grade 3 and above *First-term objective:* three minutes
at 50/60 w.p.m.

Term 1:
Week 1 Units 1–5
        Alphabet, joinings, reduction of words, single-letter words

Initial and final vowel signs
Intermediate vowels
Simple groupings
Review and recap each day
Short test – dictated words using joinings

Week 2 Review test – more help where necessary
Revision
More examples on context, writing, reading
More practice on joinings
Units 6–8
Simple sentences dictated – untimed – writing attempts from sound
Short test – dictated words on theory to date

Week 3 Consolidation
Units 9 and 10
Intensive practice on joinings and simple groupings
Progress check
Short test – dictated words on theory to date

Week 4 Revision and recap
One- and two-minute timings on thoroughly practised work
Simple sentences from sound (unseen)
Units 11 and 12 and business groupings
Short test – dictated words and groupings

Week 5 Revision and recap
Units 13, 14, 15
Consolidation exercises
Attempts at dictation on thoroughly practised material – one, two or three minutes at 30/40 w.p.m.
Simple sentences from sound (unseen)

Week 6 Revision and consolidation
Units 16, 17 (briefly), 18, 19
Complete review to date
Attempts at dictation – thoroughly practised – two to three minutes at 40 w.p.m.

Week 7 Recap – as and where necessary
Units 20 and 21
Dictation practice

Week 8 Recap – as and where necessary
Units 22 and 23
Dictation practice
Exam passages at 40/50 w.p.m. – up to three minutes, depending on difficulty
Developing word-carrying ability

Week 9 Thorough review of Units 22 and 23
Dictation practice

Recap groupings from Unit 11 plus other useful business
groupings

Exam passages at 40/50 w.p.m. – up to three minutes depending
on difficulty

Any word beginning from Units 26–29 to be dealt with as and
when they arise in dictation matter

Groupings arising out of exam passages to be thoroughly
practised

Week 10 Units 24 and 25 (parts, only as required at present)

Dictation for three minutes at 40, 50, 60 w.p.m.

Week 11 Units 26–29 (as much as required for the present)

Dictation at three minutes at 40, 50, 60 w.p.m.

Stamina-building passages on easy material – up to five minutes

Week 12 Unit 31

Dictation – three minutes at 50/60 w.p.m.

End-of-term test – transcribed passages. Student choice of 40,
50, 60 w.p.m.

Week 13 Review test

Dictation – items of seasonal interest

Teeline crossword puzzles

Shorthand 'games'

From Week 9 onwards a typed and/or hand-written transcription will
be done in class and taken in for marking. The shorthand notes will also
be handed in.

Objectives

Before preparing a syllabus, a scheme of work, a lesson or even a lesson
unit, a set of objectives must be prepared so that the teacher has a target
at which to aim. An objective implies more than an aim and should be
measurable by giving an indication of what the student will be able to
achieve at the end of the course or lesson. One way to test the
effectiveness of the teaching at the end of the learning period is by
checking through the objectives to see what has been accomplished under
the conditions laid down. The objectives are usually formulated in
behavioural terms (i.e. any classroom activity performed by the learner
that is observable by the teacher) but must also be specific and precise so
that the interpretations are narrow. They are useful in giving a clear and
concise guide to the teacher when deciding on a lesson topic and the
material and methods to be used, and they also enable an outsider to see
the purpose at a glance.

A suggested set of behavioural objectives for a first lesson in Teeline
might be such that at the end the student will be able to:

(a) **describe** James Hill's reasons for inventing and developing the
Teeline system;

(b) **use** a shorthand notebook in the prescribed manner;
(c) **write** the date at the foot of each page and **appreciate** the reasons why this is done;
(d) **assume** and **maintain** correct posture while writing;
(e) **assume** the correct position of the hands and know how to hold the writing instrument;
(f) be **conversant** with the place in the learning process of drills and repetition;
(g) **copy** outlines in the notebook from the chalkboard after demonstration;
(h) **perceive** the relationship between handwriting size and size of Teeline characters;
(i) **understand** the difference in Teeline vowels and consonants – vowels have two shapes;
(j) **develop** the rudiments of the art of writing – correct outlines, fluency, light writing touch and their interrelationship with each other;
(k) **read** from copy selected simple sentences in Teeline using the alphabet letters, single-letter words and straightforward joinings;
(l) **write** from copy selective simple sentences in Teeline using the alphabet letters, single-letter words and straightforward joinings.

In short, any change to be expected in the learning behaviour of the student should be stated as an objective. Naturally, different groups will have differing objectives.

Lesson planning

The planning and organization of a lesson is a progression of complex activities. First of all, certain points relating to the subject-matter must be deliberated.

(a) What do the students already know and what revision might be required in connection with any previous learning?
(b) What is the new topic?
(c) What will be the objectives for the lesson?
(d) What materials, teaching and learning aids will be necessary?
(e) What will be the best teaching method to use in connection with (a) and (b)?

Once some thought has been given to this, several other factors have also to be taken into consideration:

1. The 1944 Education Act stated that each student had to be educated according to age, ability and aptitude – the three As – and this state of affairs still applies. Younger students need a different approach from mature ones, slower learners will need more learning time set aside for

them than high flyers, some students have far more natural aptitude for
shorthand than others – so account must be taken of these different
categories in your lesson preparation.
2. What do you know about your students? Are they straight from
school? A second-year group already known to your colleagues from their
first year? A mixed bag with a variety of backgrounds and attainments?
3. How long is the lesson likely to last? Forty-five minutes, 1 hour, 2
hours?
4. Is the class timed for morning, afternoon or evening?
5. Where is the lesson to take place – which room, which building, or
which annexe?
6. What equipment might be available that will help visually or orally, or
will the aids be extremely basic?
7. What will be your teaching approach?

Any lesson is divided into three main parts – an introduction, a period
of full output when the effective learning takes place, and a slowing-
down period. Additionally, a shorthand lesson must contain a progression
of essential elements if it is to achieve optimum success and attain its
objectives:

1. An **introduction** in which new knowledge is built on to old; a period
of recap to enable the student to get in the correct frame of mind; and a
'warming-up' period. Drills can usefully be given here.
2. **New learning**, when the mind will be at its most receptive with
interest and motivation at their peak. This is a phase of full output with
the learner in top gear.
3. **Practice material** on the new learning.
4. **New work** presented in a dictated passage.
5. **Slowing-down phase** with output waning slowly at first and then
more rapidly. Here the teacher will be taking stock of the lesson and
whether or not the objectives have been achieved. At this point, too,
fatigue may be setting in, marked by fidgeting and talking, so a change
of activity will offer a welcome respite. Some simple dictation well within
the grasp of all the class would be beneficial to enable the lesson to finish
on a happy note with the learner feeling that progress has been made.

Effective learning requires active interest and student participation.
Boredom (where the desire to learn is very low) and fatigue (where the
student is too drained to have any wish to learn) are the enemies of
effective learning.
In order to make the best of the available learning time, the full
output phase must be as long as possible in relation to the other two, and
if lesson periods are too short there is a danger that the lesson will be
over before this phase has run its full course. The best length of lesson
time for seniors and adults is 45 minutes–1 hour, based on the premise

that the more difficult the material the shorter the effective learning time. A variety of teaching methods and aids should be used with constant checks on learning.

Lesson plan

Subject: Teeline shorthand
Objectives:
Main:

By the end of the lesson the student will understand the way in which the TR and DR blends are used and be able to apply and transfer this knowledge to a contextual and writing situtation.

Subsidiary:

1. Maintain good habits and techniques in writing.
2. Improve penmanship on groupings already learned.
3. Use key for checking.
4. Revise theory knowledge to date.
5. Incorporate previous day's homework into new learning.

Date: *Class:* 1st year day release, average
No. in class: ability
Time: (1 hour)   *Materials required:* coloured
Room no: chalks, textbook

Time	*Keyword*	*Matter and method*	*Visual aids*
5 mins	Word groupings	Drill and practise groupings from Unit 10	Difficulties on chalkboard if requested
15 mins	Dictation	Untimed dictation on Ex.51B [learnt as homework]. Check with key. Redictate at 40 and 50. Circulate during checking. Special check on student X and student Y.	
20 mins	TR blends	Teacher explanation.	TR blend in T position. TR at beginning of word *tram, trap, trail, treatment, trick, trot*
		Write shorthand outline with longhand below	T vowel R at beginning of word *tear, terror, Terence, torment* TR or T vowel R in middle or end of word *tutor, litter, doctor, mustard*

Time	Keyword	Matter and method	Visual aids
	DR blends	What can be done with T can also be done with D. Write shorthand outline with longhand below. So, what does this say (by induction)?	*dream, drench, drooping, dragon*
		What is the difference in writing position? Why?	*dorsal, darling, daringly, dearest endearment, radar, leadership, endurance, Andrew*
	Copy	Copy from board Re-copy at faster rate	
15 mins	Sentences	Ex. 53 sentences 1–4 – transcribe Ex. 54 sentences 1–3 – put into Teeline Walk round – giving help. Dictate	Textbook
5 mins	Reminder	Close class Remember – clear bits of paper, pencil shavings	
	Homework	Set homework – copy outlines from textbook Unit 11, No. 1 – make sure you understand as you write	

Studying for the course

Before embarking on the teacher's course, in addition to having the correct entry qualifications, much thought must be given to the 'domestic' angle of the course. Whatever the length of time you spend in college, you should expect to spend an average of at least 1 hour a day in home and personal study. It is really a case of saying goodbye to a hectic social life for the duration of the course and dedicating yourself to study – otherwise you are not going to give yourself the chance of success.

During the years I have been involved with teachers' certificate courses it has been proved time and time again that those students who were motivated, who got down to serious study and did the set homework plus that little bit extra, were the ones who were successful. It is extremely hard work but very satisfying, especially when the envelope comes to your home bearing a 'pass' slip.

First of all, do not attempt to study when lounging in a comfortable armchair – perhaps even in front of the television. Instead, look for the most peaceful room in your home that has a desk or table available. Make sure that all the books and documents you are likely to need are within reach so that your train of thought is not broken by constant sorties in and out of the room. It is not a good plan to study when you are tired or worried because only half your mind will be on the task in hand and you will to a large extent have wasted your time. Before attempting any new learning always look back and read the last few pages of your notes so that you have a sound foundation on which to build the new material. As a prospective teacher you are going to have considerable responsibility for ensuring that a student is in an optimum learning situation so, as charity begins at home, do correct attitudes to your own learning.

The student

As part of your course, your tutor will recommend various books on educational psychology and principles, and during the lectures will supplement this reading by examples and experiences that will help you to understand those points that you may find difficult.

It might be opportune, therefore, at this point to summarize the various types of student you are likely to meet in the course of teaching. Each student we meet is different and, as such, should be treated in an individual way.

The curve of normal distribution shows that in each class or group, the majority of people fall within the medium band of ability. There will always be one or two at the very lowest range of ability, plus one or two near geniuses, but by far the greatest number fall within the middle or average range. This curve can also be used to measure such things as physical or mental traits, laws of chance or opinion polls, and the curve always follows the same pattern. If a random sample of people being quizzed in the street for opinions on a particular product in connection with market research was analysed, the curve would still look exactly the same. It is possible, though, that in abnormal circumstances a 'skewed' curve might result, moving left or right of centre, for example, the measurement of IQs in a class of graduates would show up in this way with a one-sided bias.

Many individual differences will be found:

Educational attainment

In further education classes there is usually a wide disparity in the educational abilities of students. Sometimes an attempt is made to band students who have similar educational qualifications, e.g. O level English or its equivalent, three CSEs grades 3 and above, etc., but with the best will in the world, in days of economic stringency, college authorities have to amalgamate groups so that what appeared to be a uniform group in the first lesson might not be so after the first few weeks. Evening classes in particular suffer in this way because, by their very nature, there is a wide range of ability – perhaps a graduate or two on the one hand, and an unskilled factory worker on the other, with various stages in between. In most colleges an English aptitude test is given before a student enrols on a shorthand course, certainly on a full-time course, but the possession of a lower-grade CSE in English does not mean that there is an adequate command of the English language to cope with transcription, although this is often taken as sufficient entry qualification for a part-time or evening shorthand course. So often skill subjects are dismissed as being an easy option – the idea that 'any fool can learn to type/write shorthand' is still quite commonplace among academics. People are often accepted for a shorthand course with insufficient educational background so, whether we personally are in favour of this or not, they have to be taught and trained to the best of their ability.

Manual dexterity

After a learner has been writing shorthand 'outlines' for only a few hours it is possible to see who has a natural aptitude for the physical movements of writing shapes. Some people write beautiful, flowing outlines that are readable and recognizable from the outset, while others, however good their writing instrument, appear to be writing with a poker. Given demonstration and practice, the majority of learners eventually write a more pleasing style of shorthand but it can take a considerable number of hours before this is achieved. During the theory-learning stage, once the alphabetic letters are automatized, some part of each lesson must be devoted to the art of writing and the development of manual dexterity until an acceptable style is established.

Personality

Introverts and extroverts

Our students differ in the way they exhibit extremes of personality traits. Some will be open and extrovert, others quiet and introvert, with the rest of the group slotted in between at various points along the scale – a good example of how one could apply the curve of normal distribution. Extroverts are friendly and sociable, almost cheeky, and can be useful members of the class if you win them over to your side and channel their interests in the right direction. Introverts are rather shy and reserved, keep themselves to themselves, and are often immersed in their own thoughts. Introverts in the classroom sometimes get overlooked because they usually get on with their appointed tasks quietly, unwilling to draw attention to themselves. Extroverts are their mirror image whose names we always know from the outset and who persist in their demands until they get attention. Care must be taken to give these two widely different class members their fair share of teacher attention – introverts not being pushed aside at the expense of their more extrovert neighbour, each one being treated according to their own personality. The extrovert usually shines in question and answer sessions, while the introvert (who may previously have been considered rather dull) often does well in tests, proving that individuals have different ways of learning and applying themselves.

Temperament

The age when a student enters the further-education sector usually corresponds with the age of wanting independence from the parental home. This is the time when some students are expressing their approach to adulthood via way-out hairstyles and dress. We must not judge them on appearance alone, because often a pleasant surprise is in store and a really charming personality is hidden beneath the garish appearance. Students are people in their own right and as such their ideas and personalities must be respected, even though they might not coincide with our own. Some students are very emotional and will react easily to real or imagined problems, while others put on an aggressive front and are immediately on the defensive when called to task. Students generally are co-operative if they have an aim in view and can see the reason for a task being attempted in a particular way. They enjoy being treated as adults and usually accept criticism and fair comment cheerfully. The student's own attitude to learning, college life and the teaching staff is also important – students straight from school feel they have achieved a degree of maturity in an adult world.

Concentration

Differences in concentration are less obvious at first sight and this appears to have little to do with ability or intellect. In the Teeline class students who at the theory stage have the promise of being good shorthand writers because they do their homework and concentrate on copying and reading, sadly do not always fulfil the early promise. They still try, and work hard at the speed stage but with only moderate and limited results, in direct contrast to students with a great deal of ability who sail through the learning stage without appearing to put in much effort. Intelligent students in the main make better shorthand writers although English ability is a vital element; however, it does not follow that someone with a high IQ automatically becomes a high-speed writer.

The ceiling may be reached at 80 w.p.m., but differences in writing, aptitude and reasons for learning shorthand are sufficient to bring about this anomaly.

Special aptitudes

Intelligence, as shown by IQ tests, is known as the 'General' or 'G' factor, but individuals differ in the amount of 'Special' or 'S' factors also present in their make-up. Special factors include memory, verbal and mechanical facility, manual dexterity, mathematical ability or musical and artistic talent. It can thus be seen that the possession of several 'S' factors are necessary qualities of a shorthand writer and also how their presence or absence can account for widely differing speed attainments. 'S' factors can also be developed within certain limits by training and a caring, stimulating teaching environment.

Differences in sexes

Although secretarial work has tended to be female orientated since the end of the First World War, neither sex has any particular advantage when it comes to learning these skills. Both men and women are equally skilled as shorthand writers and although women have a slight physical advantage at learning keyboard skills (i.e. in the main their hands and fingers are not as broad) successful high-speed court reporters are made up of members of both sexes. Secretarial skills classes are attended largely by females, but classes for journalists and police cadets are more evenly balanced.

Social background

Students come from a wide variety of homes and educational establishments. Colleges in particular cater for students from quite a wide geographical area so a truly comprehensive cross-section of the community appears in the classrooms. Some students come from socially disadvantaged backgrounds and they tend to be less articulate and sometimes more lacking in politeness than those from more privileged homes. It is quite gratifying to see that generally students rub shoulders quite amicably and become part of a homogeneous group under the guidance of a well-motivated teacher. Many students from ethnic minority groups have special needs and the sympathetic teacher should be aware of this.

In conclusion, we must remember that the training and well-being of the student should be first and foremost in our scale of teaching priorities. Everyone has some redeeming feature and often the less-intelligent students have the more pleasant natures. The student is the paramount concern and administrative work, marking, lesson plans are only secondary, for without the student they would merely be an end to a means.

Principles of learning

It might be appropriate at this stage to formulate a definition of learning and the difference between learning and teaching. A simple dictionary definition cites learning as 'a progressive change in behaviour', and teaching provides the conditions in which effective learning takes place.

Learning can never be a passive process but always an active one. There must be a desire to acquire knowledge by the learner as it cannot manifest itself by some kind of magical transfer from teacher to learner. Each of us learns at a different rate in an individual way. The road to learning is not smooth but has a series of peaks in the form of fast spurts, followed by periods when learning appears to be stationary – although in reality consolidation is taking place.

A common misconception on the part of the trainee teacher is that after entering the classroom one writes on the chalkboard what one would like the group to do in the next hour or so, and then the students respond without delay or fuss by getting on with the set work with no further explanation. Then, at the end of the lesson the work produced is handed in correct and free from error. Oh, how wrong can one be and how far from the truth! Teaching is not like that at all.

During the years I have been involved with teachers' courses, I have asked my trainee students what they can remember about their own learning days and in the main this is what would-be teachers remember or think they remember of their own training. After discussion, we have concluded that looking at a lesson through a student's eyes (perhaps only a few years earlier) is quite a different proposition when viewed from a teaching point of view in the hands of a well-trained skills teacher. I can hardly imagine that any self-respecting skills teacher ever taught shorthand and typing in such a manner, even in the days before training colleges were established.

Components in the learning process

Intelligence

Reference has already been made to the 'G' factor – intelligence. The more intelligent the students, the easier they will find it to relate given rules and examples in shorthand to similar situations occurring later in the theory. For instance, when building up speed an intelligent student, having been taught the principle of *each, much, such, which*, will apply this to such words as *catch* and *teach* and, what is more, have the necessary ability to transcribe them safely and speedily. Less intelligent students will be unable to work this out for themselves, merely copying what they have been given earlier and being less likely to attempt their own word groupings on a trial-and-error basis.

Age

Between the ages of 16 and 18, students should be at the peak of their learning powers. However, learning ability decreases with age, so it is harder for mature students to learn the mechanics of shorthand even though they are well motivated and keen to learn. Teeline is an excellent system from this point of view and, if the necessary writing facility can be attained, is likely to be very successful.

Motivation

Motivation, or drive, is selective and organized action. It is stimulated by curiosity, which is a desire to learn (often by problem-solving and reasoned arguments); however, in unsettled learning conditions the motivating forces can be extinguished, with boredom taking its place. If motivation is the zenith of learning, then boredom is the nadir giving rise to tedium, lack of drive and an unwillingness to learn. The moral is for the teacher to make use of the motivation forces and establish a sound student/teacher relationship, while endeavouring to ascertain from the beginning of the course what general reasons the students have for learning shorthand and their personal and specific aims.

In the main the reasons fall into four main divisions:

(a) To gain qualifications in the expectation that at the end of the course the student will find a well-paid post that gives job satisfaction.

(b) Parental pressure is put on some young students to gain secretarial qualifications if the parents see office work as offering a better start to life than they had themselves and to whom a 'white-collar' nine-to-five job appeals. Some students confide that as their mothers once worked in an office, this has motivated them to try for this type of career.

(c) To train while looking for a job, even though the job they eventually take is not office work. They may have aspirations towards nursing or the Forces when old enough, but they see the skills subjects as always being of use at a later stage in their lives.

(d) Evening students in particular are often motivated to improve their abilities for reasons of personal satisfaction. They may be updating their knowledge, or a married woman may enjoy the chance of an evening out with a similar-minded friend while her husband babysits – and also have the bonus of proficiency in a skill at the end of the course. Some students are merely interested in Teeline as a note-taking device for use in lectures or in some hobby they may have.

Motivation can be stimulated by the teacher in encouraging the students to think objectively – in times of high unemployment it is always the better qualified student who gets an interview. Interest can be maintained by short talks on the teacher's own business experiences, positions available in the Forces or abroad, looking for advertised positions in the local and national Press, and the necessity for linking shorthand to new technology.

Competitions are another way of arousing interest. This can mean competition against peers or against oneself, the latter being when one strives to improve on a previous personal best. Learning can be either intrinsic, in which learning is undertaken because one likes the pursuit of knowledge with no external reward (primary learning), or extrinsic, in which the learner might be working for an examination, a prize, or even for praise in addition to the skills or information gathered (secondary). Praise can be a good motivating force, enjoyed by children and adults alike, and helps to establish rapport in the classroom.

Reinforcement

With young children any learnt activity that is rewarded brings perseverance, but if the activity is ignored it tends to disappear. During question and answer sessions, if the teacher tends always to choose the same children to answer, the others in the class quickly lose interest because they know they will not be able to impart what they know for the teacher's approval and the approval of the rest of the group. This desire for recognition largely disappears with maturity and further-education students do not always want to answer and draw attention to themselves in front of the rest of the class. They do not wish to be found wanting when answering and have sometimes to be encouraged and wheedled into reading back after note-taking.

Success

Success and confidence in the reading of a shorthand note encourages the student to try harder. Success builds on success, failure breeds failure. Speed targets should be set that can be seen to be realistic and obtainable by the student. There is no point in attempting a speed that the student sees as impossible, but at the same time there should always be the thrill of a challenge. The setting of too high a target speed leads to discouragement and lack of effort. Too low a challenge will impede progress and lead to a static situation.

Knowledge of results

Before improvement in learning is forthcoming, the student needs to be aware of errors made in either:

(a) the shorthand note, leading to a faulty transcription;
(b) in the transcription itself;
(c) carelessness in either (a) or (b) above;
(d) errors in English;
(e) errors in memory, confusion of shorthand outlines, transpositions;
(f) errors of recall, perhaps because of only partially written outlines.

The results need to be analysed so that the student can correct and rectify the faults made.

Results may appear as either:

(a) an end score only, with a mark at the end of the transcript. If the transcript is well-nigh perfect the learner can draw his/her own conclusions from the mark which serves as a concise summary of performance; but if the end score is less than 100 per cent the student has no means of knowing exactly what went wrong; or
(b) with the advantage of feedback. The earlier this can be done after completion of the transcript the more beneficial. Immediate feedback is not always possible, when homework has been given in for marking, for instance.

Written comments in addition to a 'mark' should be included, together with suggestions for what can be done to bring about an improvement in performance, plus a few minutes spent with each student – even if this might have to be shared on a cyclical basis if this is all that time permits. Regretfully there is always a small band of students only interested in the mark itself, so care should be taken to see that they read the comments you have made in order to benefit from them even if you do not manage to have a word personally each lesson.

This provides not only learning feedback (i.e. what the student should have done) but also action feedback (i.e. what needs to be done next).

During the actual practice period in a lesson, comments, board work, facility drills and further examples, all provide students with information leading to the development of the correct stimulus bonds, thus helping to eliminate errors and letting them know how their performance compares with the objectives in mind.

Thorndike's famous laws suggest that the three most important essentials to learning are:

(a) the Law of Readiness, by having a correctly prepared mind, continuously applied;
(b) the Law of Use, by continually making and remaking stimulus-response bonds; and
(c) the Law of Effect, which gives an ongoing feeling of well-being and satisfaction as a result of (a) and (b).

In shorthand the Law of Effect will show as a well-written transcript with accuracy of more than 96 per cent and the comfortable feeling of being able to make use of one's shorthand note with confidence in order to achieve this desirable position.

The learning process

Learning falls into two main groups: *unconscious*, or unknowing, which the student acquires unwittingly without conscious effort; *conscious*, or deliberate, which requires a conscious effort on the part of the student.

Unconscious learning can be influenced by the type of learning material the teacher uses, by the atmosphere created in the classroom and the attitudes shown and developed by the teacher.

Conscious learning falls into several sub-groups:

Learning by doing

This is by far the most important way of learning skill subjects. Swimming, driving a car or playing the guitar cannot be learned simply by having the various parts explained and then being left to one's own devices. However adept and interested, some degree of practice would be necessary before the skill can be perfected and the practice would not be effective if one had no idea of the correct movements or the most economical way of making them. Students need to have the correct way of writing shorthand explained briefly, then demonstrated, and then these movements perfected by practice. The movements should be broken down into their various components where necessary, then speeded up into normal writing speed which is increased by controlled and effective practice. The stimulus in a shorthand lesson is the spoken word; the response is the correct shorthand note obtained by the short circuiting of the learning track in the brain, thereby encouraging the formation of stimulus-response bonds.

Explanation in the shorthand class should be as brief as possible, meaningful and to the point, with the bulk of the lesson spent on activities by the student in writing or reading Teeline. Constant practice ensures that the stimulus-response bonds are automatized and formed without conscious thinking. If the students are sitting inactively, merely listening to long pontifications on the part of the teacher, they become bored because no effort is required of them and their attention wanders. Interest and curiosity play a great part in learning and if these are not stimulated learning is not taking place.

Learning by imitation

Imitation has a major part to play in learning a skill. It is one of the basic learning methods and can be observed during the first year of life as, for instance, when babies imitate adults by smiling or clapping hands. Once students have watched the teacher writing the shorthand symbols, their interest is roused and they are keen to imitate and produce their own early attempts. Therefore the onus is on teachers to ensure that their own model strokes are correct for students will not only assimilate the correct movements, but also incorporate any incorrect movements as well.

For example, a letter C written carelessly on the largish side can be misconstrued as a letter L and this shape is copied in all innocence by the beginner student. We learn by imitation, so let the tutor beware and ensure that what is being imitated is what was intended.

The golden rules are:

(a) students imitate correct movements after being shown how and why (demonstration);
(b) movements should be written initially at correct speed, then broken down if necessary into slow motion and later written again at normal writing speed;
(c) practice should then take place under supervision; and finally
(d) directed practice when the student is free to consolidate the newly acquired movements.

Once bad habits are allowed to develop they are most difficult to eliminate because when speed-building is under way in earnest, the student is so anxious to develop this that the wrong movements are intensified in an effort to get the 'take'. It is very easy to spot who in the class is writing in a peculiar way. Unfortunately some students reach the shorthand room with badly developed handwriting techniques and there is little that can be done to rectify this if the writing instrument has been held incorrectly for several years.

Once the stimulus-response bond has been developed, students will have settled into their own pattern of writing and after this point has been reached there is little benefit from demonstration. Certainly methods of writing outlines should be shown upon request or where there is likely to be difficulty, and teachers can demonstrate their own method of writing – but this is purely for informative purposes.

Learning by rote

This plays no part at all in learning a skill. While the formation of good working habits should be inculcated into the students, skills, as mentioned earlier, are learned by doing and demonstration in the early stages. The nearest in shorthand to any repetitive learning is perhaps by using facility drills, but even this is overshadowed by the fact that students are really participating in developing the skill.

Lecture

This plays no part in learning a skill. It is suitable for conveying information to large groups where time may be limited, but the group is not participating unless time is given at the end for asking questions. The lecture is more formal than other methods of teaching.

Discussion

Question and answer can be used to good effect here, but a discussion itself is of extremely limited use in learning a skill except for a few minutes of liberalization during a lesson when information might be given on something that may crop up in a dictation passage.

Role play

This is no use in a shorthand lesson but can be valuable in office practice and communication skills and perhaps composing a letter in transcription if this is in the syllabus, or if time permits. This is an informal method of teaching and contrasts sharply with the lecture.

Learning by appointment

This is an economical method of learning both from the point of view of time and money. Students attend college at set hours to suit their own convenience and work from specially prepared tapes or some other learning device at their own pace. Time is set aside for advice and/or practical help, but in the main students are responsible for their own learning situation. This method can be very useful to the learner in a speed-building situation or on keyboard training in conjunction with computer technology.

Programmed learning

Information is presented in a 'programme' – a type of workbook, or video frame, through which learners will progress at their own speed. A programme might consist of a short piece of theory learning (e.g. cheques in office practice) or a whole topic – as in the many commercial series available. One of the dangers here is that motivation might be lost and interest wane.

Retention and recall

Retention is the ability to retain and store facts, but it is an unconscious process. Some facts unable to be recalled to mind at a certain time are obviously retained because they can be produced from memory at a later date without any apparent effort being made, thus proving that human beings retain far more than can be recalled.

Recall is the ability to select the information required upon demand. Forgetting is an inability to recall rather than an inability to retain. Perhaps a word grouping or a learning principle which momentarily escapes us can suddenly be remembered when a similar grouping is being used, triggering off a memory chain and showing evidence that the knowledge had been retained even though it could not be recalled earlier.

To improve retention, revision must be continued throughout the course. As Teeline is so easy to learn, revision need not be so intensive as with some other shorthand systems, but nevertheless it can be very profitable when used in connection with speed-building activities and also immediately after the principles have been introduced.

At an early stage of learning the system – when dealing with joinings, let us say – meaningful joinings are retained better than nonsense joinings. Joinings that suggest words (rather than those which in the English language would never occur together) should be given so that practice material is meaningful and also learned to the point of automaticity. This is known as 'over-learning' and as such will be retained, even though there is no knowledge of the act of retention and, what is more, recall will be immediate. Distributed practice is an aid to retention – 1 hour of shorthand each day, five times a week, is retained infinitely better than longer periods at infrequent intervals.

The original learning must be efficient and effective, otherwise recall cannot take place. Recall is dependent upon the recency and frequency of the learning, revision or recapitulation, and connecting the various items of information together.

Memory

Memory span is the amount of information that can be remembered accurately. It increases rapidly during childhood, an innate ability being developed to remember more complex and larger amounts of material for longer periods. Material to be held in the memory has first to be learned (e.g. the Teeline alphabet), secondly, it has to be retained (till next lesson in the early learning stages) and thirdly, it has to be remembered (indefinitely) and finally automatized (stimulus-response bonds formed).

The unconscious use of imagery is an aid to memory. Things can be brought to mind by visualizing where an event took place, or by hearing certain stimuli a forgotten event can be recalled. One can imagine and visualize shorthand outlines in the air while perhaps riding on a bus or sitting in the bath, thus helping to fix the shapes in our minds.

Memory decreases with age. Happenings that occurred in the distant past can often be recalled with vivid clarity by elderly people when events of last week have not been retained at all. Imagery, too, tends to decrease with age – the adult with experience of life usually relying instead on concepts and the retention of facts.

So-called 'poor' memories are a bit of a misnomer, as it is not the memory that is poor but that the recall ability is momentarily at fault. Sometimes we have the feeling of not being able to remember something that we ought to be able to recall immediately – a feeling of annoyance that the information is 'at the back of our minds' or 'on the tip of our tongues', thus showing that retention has definitely taken place but recall is temporarily lacking.

Human beings retain much more information than they believe they do. Much trivial information that is apparently absorbed is of necessity forgotten in due course, otherwise our brains would contain so much information that the finest computer ever developed would appear as simple as an abacus.

Qualities of the teacher

Subject and educational knowledge

Teachers should have a solid foundation of teaching sensory motor skills with a thorough knowledge of skill techniques. They must be proficient in the skill of shorthand, knowing Teeline inside out. As a result of this, they will understand students' problems having gone through the learning mill themselves. All the means at teachers' disposal should be used to teach Teeline in an imaginative way, using visual aids wherever possible.

Personality

A friendly, pleasant manner with unlimited patience should be a prerequisite, someone who will always be willing to lend a sympathetic ear but at the same time be firm if the occasion demands it. Everyone should be treated in the same way – no favouritism, no sarcasm, no apparent 'picking' on a student, but still respecting each one's individuality. There should be no suggestion of a vastly superior being, but the teacher should be known as someone who is approachable and not afraid to admit to human frailty if caught out. Always promise to find out the answer if you are unable to deal with a question and then do not forget to follow it up. In addition, do not take sides or get too involved in the students' personal lives, lest this be seen as prying. Teachers are responsible for a happy relationship with students, and the atmosphere of the class will reflect the teacher's personality. So be sure that what you do is of a standard worth copying.

Mannerisms

A clean and tidy appearance should be presented. Avoid mannerisms such as taking one's spectacles off and on, or twiddling with stray tufts of hair. This type of habit is not only distracting but can also become a target for imitation and ridicule. Speech should be loud enough to be heard from the back of the room with clear enunciation – even with an accent, local, regional or otherwise.

Understanding

The ability to give a proper demonstration and explanation must be developed. High standards must be set and also learning how to judge how much information the student can absorb in a given time.

Discipline

Never attempt to teach until you have the attention of all in the room. Students eventually become aware that you are waiting to speak and this awareness progresses steadily until all the voices tail off. It is a far more effective way than trying to shout over the noise of their chatter. Instructions should be given one at a time, repeating them if necessary.

There is always someone who is not really listening but it should be apparent that you are the leader, taking the initiative and intending your instructions to be followed. A formal approach is best when first meeting a new group, and then when one has sized up the group (and this also includes the need the group has to assess you) discipline can be relaxed somewhat, although not to the extent of permitting too much familiarity and lack of courtesy.

Keeping students busy ensures an orderly class, which is one element in keeping a harmonious atmosphere. Develop a roving eye that will penetrate all corners of the room and never make idle threats or promises that will be impossible to fulfil.

Enthusiasm

Last but not least, always appear to be an enthusiastic and cheerful figure. This is infectious and the mood will be passed on to the student. Have a positive attitude and encourage your students to enjoy Teeline for its own sake as well as for any future benefits it might bring.

Class management

1. At the beginning of the session it is a wise plan to give a short talk about the course, its objectives, the layout and practical details of the

establishment and also what is expected of students behaviourwise and their attitudes to staff and fellow students.

2. Students should be trained to get out their notebooks and pencils as soon as they are seated in the room and start to write shorthand (perhaps work from the last lesson), word groupings, outlines from theory books, alphabetic drills etc., which will act not only as a warm-up for the lesson but form part of the regular practice needed to build up a skill. If the importance and value of this are explained by the teacher at the beginning of the session it becomes a good habit, a form of self-discipline, and will eventually transfer over to an office situation.

A theory book is indispensable in the early stages and I suggest a small book with alphabetic cut-outs on the right-hand side – an address book will suffice – in which groupings, unusual or special outlines can be written as they occur and used as facility drills at the beginning of a lesson. These facility drills can be used by the teacher as a warm-up, timed or untimed, and eventually this leads to a tidying-up of outline length and size in the student's notebook.

The lesson should be finished five minutes before time so that students have time to put things away and go off to their next lesson, which means that any incoming teacher to the room can also start the next lesson on time. This courtesy does not mean that every minute should not count in the shorthand lesson because it is vital that it should.

3. Although this suggestion is out of the scope of the individual teacher, each full-time student should have a locker where personal equipment can be kept. Coats should be hung on any hooks provided in the classroom and bags and parcels must not be left in the aisles, leaving a clear way in case of emergency.

4. Never, ever, enter the classroom unprepared. It is far better and safer and will earn the respect of the students to have more material prepared than will be used.

5. In a school or college situation there is always a certain amount of administrative work that has to be completed by the teacher. Registers must be marked each lesson and in most establishments these have to be totalled up at the end of the term and again at the end of the session when percentages, average attendances, etc. are worked out.

Absentees must be chased up personally or via a senior tutor. Students who attend a college in a day-release capacity may also need to have a report for the employer submitted at intervals and also a note sent to the firm of any absences. Evening students can be contacted by sending a postcard or telephoning them at home, perhaps after the second absence. It should be understood by students that they must explain the reason for absence on return – in general terms – and this should be made clear in the opening remarks at the beginning of the session.

6. Always insist that a student has a tidy and uncluttered work space

with any rubbish, pencil shavings or scrap paper being placed in the bin and not dropped on the floor.

7. A check should be made that the correct date appears on the chalkboard – preferably with the month written in Teeline.

8. A record of work and a marking book are essential (see Chapter 15) and a careful note kept of any examination papers that have been worked.

9. Safety Precautions. Make sure you are familiar with the fire exits and the drill for evacuating the building. Any electric machine or equipment should be switched off after use and the plugs removed from the sockets. Electric flexes on equipment should not be allowed to trail on the floor where people have to walk. All the drawers in a vertical filing cabinet should not be opened at the same time. Clamp down immediately on smoking in non-smoking areas.

10. If a student is ill, s/he should be sent to the nurse or the sickroom in the company of a fellow student, or (depending on the severity of the illness) you may have to deal with this yourself. If there has been any involvement in an accident, however slight, an accident form must be completed.

Classroom equipment

It is a fact of life that much excellent teaching is done in far from ideal conditions, in dingy rooms and with improvised furniture and equipment; but if you are asked to discuss equipment in an examination question, the examiner will be looking for the ideal. It would be very helpful, therefore, if would-be teachers could visit a well-equipped shorthand unit so that they can get a concept of what teaching conditions should be like.

Ideally the room should be light and airy with strategically placed windows and good natural and artificial lighting. The room should be in a quiet part of the building with good acoustics. Each student should have the use of a desk with a flat top about 28–30 inches (71–76 cm) from the floor and a chair with back support that is the right height for the desks. If the desks are placed in a semicircle round the teacher's table, the students will be well placed for observing and hearing the teacher, and this makes for a more informal setting than desks in rows. There should be enough room between the desks for the student to move without being cramped and for the teacher to walk round and observe. The room should be in a neat and tidy condition with the teacher setting a personal example in having a well-organized desk. Cupboards and shelves should be placed at various points around the walls together with display boards. A washbasin is a necessary accessory to encourage neat and tidy work.

Transcription must of necessity take place in a typing room and this is sometimes used as the shorthand room as well. Desks should be of the type that allows flat space for writing in shorthand notebooks, and electric points should be installed nearby for typewriters and other electrical equipment.

Such mundane articles as a waste-paper basket, board rubber and coloured chalks should not be overlooked, nor the shorthand teacher's 'badge of office', the stopwatch. Whatever the type of accommodation the would-be teacher has available, classroom organization and management should follow an ordered, well-adjusted pattern.

Teaching aids

Chalkboard

One of the best visual aids is one of the oldest – the chalkboard. A modern-type roller board can be adjusted to suit teaching conditions and many of these are a dull green colour that is restful to the eye. Yellow chalk is said to be the perfect foil for a green board, but I think that white chalk, especially for shorthand symbols, has a more pristine appearance. The board can be ruled during manufacture for music or for shorthand or can have maps drawn for commerce or geography. For shorthand beginners at least part of the board should have ruled lines because they find the Teeline easier to read this way and it ensures that the new teacher will have a parallel and tidy presentation. The student can see the lesson being developed in a logical order and different coloured chalks can be used for emphasis.

When writing on the board the habit of standing sideways should be acquired so that the back is not turned to the class nor the effect given of talking to the board. The chalk should be held lightly using a medium-sized piece. Good chalkboard work provides a summary of the lesson which can be used for recap if desired.

The disadvantage of the chalkboard is not in the board itself but in the writing medium used – chalk is rather messy, but this is only a minor problem. Always make sure you clean the board at the end of the class.

Overhead projector

An overhead projector is very useful in the shorthand room because previously prepared transparencies can be shown to the students, but it is essential when using these that students should be able to see during the lesson period how the outlines have been formed. It is possible to write on separate sheets in class but a more practical idea is to write on a transparent roll which is rotated across the projector so that students can see the teacher actually writing on the surface while she is facing the class. The light is reflected behind and hand movements show up very clearly.

The overhead projector has a particular part to play in a shorthand laboratory where chalk dust might be a hazard to sensitive equipment. When required, complicated drawings and diagrams can be photocopied and a transparency made from the photocopy. Transparencies can be framed and labelled for easy storage and handling, thus giving a permanent record.

The disadvantages are only minor. The projectors are apt to get hot and emit a slight buzzing noise. Special pens are needed but these are obtainable quite cheaply in a wide range of colours. A convenient electric point is necessary and obviously one is limited by the size and shape of the room. It is a simple matter to project on to a plain wall if a screen is not available.

Closed-circuit television and video

If these facilities exist on the college premises, a very professional presentation with an appropriate commentary can be made to emphasize such points as posture, using the notebook to best effect, facility drills formation, fast writing demonstrations, etc. These can provide a welcome break in a long lesson. Another idea is to show such a film to more than one class at a time in a lecture theatre, perhaps at the end or beginning of term. A relevant questionnaire sheet should be provided for students to complete and this can be used as a summary at the end of the lesson.

Charts

Posters stressing posture, word groupings or in effect anything that needs to be drawn to the attention of the student, can be prepared and put on the wall. They should however be changed frequently, perhaps after a fortnight, otherwise they lose impact and simply become part of the furniture and general background.

Textbooks

All students should have a copy of *Teeline Revised Edition* whether they have to buy their own or have a college copy on loan. This is a standard textbook on Teeline and it is important that candidates working for the RSA Teacher's Certificate in Shorthand (Teeline) follow the same line of theory so that the system is standardized, thus eliminating hybrid systems developed by some practising teachers.

Handouts

Well-prepared handouts in the early learning stages provide a worthwhile source of reading material and give an insight into different writing styles.

Oral aids

When it is apparent that some students are forging ahead, cassette players should be available with individual headphones. It is not necessary to have sufficient for each member of the class, because one group could be using these to work at their own pace while the rest are working with the teacher. In an ideal situation, a shorthand laboratory, any commercially-prepared listening equipment or using prepared shorthand tapes in the audio room all cater for differences in learning rates. A tape recorder used at the front of the room gives a variety of voices and a judicious change in the learning situation. It can also be useful in cases where the teacher may have a heavy cold and is in danger of losing her/his voice.

Leaflets and advertising material

These are a boon in office arts teaching generally but not specifically relevant in teaching shorthand.

Class, group and individual teaching

Class teaching

When the whole class is working together under the control of the teacher, class teaching can be said to be taking place. The class is taught as a whole with everyone working at the same pace, regardless of ability; therefore everyone is at the same level of learning. Of necessity, the teaching is aimed at the middle of the class with the result that the pace is too slow for some who are not being challenged sufficiently and too fast for others who get out of their depth and lose heart.

Class teaching is economical in the time and effort put in by the teacher and provided individual progress is not impeded can be used to advantage by saving constant repetition. It provides a method of bringing a class together after having been split into groups, for lecturing or for expounding a principle using the chalkboard or other visual method.

In teaching shorthand class teaching is a good method at the theory stage, but as individuals learn at different rates, before many weeks have passed there will be a wide disparity of speeds, some students needing to be pushed and others coaxed.

Group teaching

Once the students are at different learning stages and have to be catered for, the class can be split into groups so that each member of the group is at a similar level of learning. Groups should be limited to not more than three per class, otherwise management of the groups becomes cumbersome and each group does not get its fair quota of the teacher's time. As each group must be kept fully occupied when the teacher's attention is elsewhere, it takes a lot of organization and thought on the part of the teacher. The groups can be brought together at intervals, e.g. at the beginning or end of the lesson. This system works very well in infant schools when children are being taught to read. In a shorthand class loosely defined speed groups can be formulated, with movement up and down as necessary within the framework of class teaching.

Individual teaching

This really has no place on a skills course unless a teacher is working with one or two students only (tutorials) in a lunch break or during other free time. In a normal-sized class it is quite impractical, as students would get two or three minutes of the teacher's time in one fell swoop with no more attention for the rest of the lesson, and remain sitting, chatting or engaged in their own pursuits. This is not to say that individual teaching is not necessary occasionally, either within a group or within a class, to assist with individual difficulties.

Team teaching

A relatively new concept in teaching and a viable alternative to the normal position of one teacher being responsible for setting up a learning situation for one class of students (see Chapter 16).

Remedial teaching

This is a method of teaching pupils with 'learning disabilities' – from slow learners to those classified as retarded. Normal methods are adapted to meet individual requirements within the school. In a college, general foundation courses cater for this type of student.

Transfer of training

Let us now consider the effect previously learned skills will have on new learning. How is this learning carried over? It used to be said that if an academically inclined student was taught Latin or maths, then by concentrating on these two subjects, it would be easier to learn subjects such as chemistry or geography which have a relationship between the first two. Likewise if mathematical ability can be used in a physics lesson to work out a complex calculation, transfer of the mathematical learning has taken place. A pianist usually finds the typewriting keyboard presents no difficulties so far as flexibility of the fingers is concerned, and a fast hand-writer generally finds the transition to writing Teeline symbols quickly can be made without undue struggle.

This application of previous experience to facilitate a new learning situation is known as **positive transfer**. The opposite, **negative transfer**, occurs where past learning and experience interferes with the learning at present taking place. Errors in perception often occur and what might be perfectly clear to the teacher is often misunderstood by the student. The mention of a 'manual' typewriter to beginner students is often not seen as the opposite of an electric one unless specifically explained. Even the word 'manual' itself, in relation to the typewriter, is often repeated in speech in various forms.

Transfer is an intricate process and sometimes it does not occur in circumstances that would appear conducive. A successful tennis player does not always make a good squash or badminton player, although all are played with opponents in a court. One reason is that the methods of playing are different, the strokes are different and good team work does not replace ability and know-how.

Learning a second foreign language can interfere with the fluency of the first, even more so when the languages are similar. In motor skills learning a second shorthand system is inhibited by knowledge of a first because the stimulus-response bonds have been formed to the point of overlearning. Someone who was really proficient at the first system has far more difficulty than the person who has only a smattering of knowledge.

When a car driver has to get used to the controls of a different car her/his reactions are automatically adjusted to the car to which s/he is accustomed and deliberate thought will have to be given to the new movements until the new stimulus-response bonds are formed and, even then, under stress or panic the old movements spring to the fore.

Sometimes it is difficult to see whether there is any transfer at all. Take the case of training to use a word processor or computer keyboard. A capable typist may be expected to do well, but in reality the latter keyboards are more complex and good habits have to be unlearned; it being impossible to use the control key and the shift key at the same time with one hand as both appear at the same side of the keyboard. Again a really proficient typist would have more difficulty with the transfer than one who is not a 'touch' typist in the real sense of the word.

When timetables are being prepared care should be taken to see that two similar subjects are not taught consecutively, Spanish followed by

Italian or book-keeping followed by accounts, particularly if different teachers are involved.

For positive transfer to take place there should be a common denominator between the two subjects and the student should be really adept at the first. Transfer can be improved if the student is aware of the link between the two. One of the reasons for teaching desirable working habits in office arts classes is that this will instinctively result in positive transfer to a working situation.

Teaching practice

Finally, although this is one of the most important parts of the teachers' course, I would like to give teachers some encouragement for the 10 hours or more spent in the classroom for teaching practice. Candidates always dread the thought of taking over someone's class and I sympathize; because it is a nerve-wracking experience not being sure exactly what the students know or at what rate individuals are able to learn.

The teaching experience will be arranged in several blocks throughout the two years and while you may think that your teaching will never improve, I can assure you that it will, and by the time your last lessons are taking place you will be enjoying it.

This is achieved by helpful comment and constructive criticism on the part of the teacher whose class you are taking initially, and later by the course tutor. The vast majority of members of college teaching staffs are only too ready to help would-be teachers because they can remember when they themselves were in a similar situation and will make allowances for your inexperience.

Your tutor will probably give you a written report on your performance designed to help in your next teaching session, followed by a tutorial in which difficulties can be aired.

Before going into the class situation opportunity will be given for observing the class being taken by its normal teacher. Arrangements might also be made for you to see a video film of a lesson given by an experienced teacher, or, if facilities are available, you may take part in a short class session of filming and when it is re-run later you will be able to judge for yourself what your strong and weak points are. You should find this a tremendous help.

Some points to remember about teaching practice:

Try to project your voice and do not address your remarks to the chalkboard.

The board should contain a summary of your lesson with a heading and date.

Hand-outs should be as near perfect as possible – free from spelling errors and ambiguities, relevant, up to date and well presented.

Have prepared a well-structured lesson plan based on age, ability and aptitude of the students.

Always arrive in the classroom in good time before the commencement of the lesson so that you have time to write what you need on the board and get your mind attuned to the task in hand.

Good management and organization come with experience, but teaching method is very personal and can vary enormously between individuals with each method having something to recommend it.

I hope these remarks have been of some help. Good luck in your teaching career!

Further reading

D. Barnes, J. Britton and H. Rosen, *Language, the Learner and the School* (Penguin, 1969).

B. Bernstein, *Class, Codes and Control*, Vols 1–3 (Routledge & Kegan Paul, 1977, 1973 and 1977).

R. Borger and A. Seaborne, *Psychology of Learning* (Penguin, 1970).

L. Curzon, *Teaching in Further Education* (Cassell, 1976).

L. Derville, *Use of Psychology in Teaching* (Longman, 1966).

L. Douglas *et al.*, *Teaching Business Subjects* (Prentice-Hall, 1972).

Dept of Education and Science, *A Language for Life*, the Bullock Report (HMSO, 1975).

Dept of Education and Science, *Youth Training Scheme: Implications for the Education Service*, Circular 6/82 (September, 1982).

P. Fitts and M. Posner, *Human Performance* (Greenwood Press, 1979).

L. Gartside, *Teaching Business Subjects* (Macdonald and Evans, 1970).

E. Hilgard and R. Atkinson, *Introduction to Psychology* (Harcourt Brace Jovanovich, 1975).

I. Hill and M. Bowers, *Teeline Revised Edition* (Heinemann Educational Books, 1983).

A. Hughes and E. Hughes, *Learning and Teaching* (Longman, n.d.).

K. Lovell, *Educational Psychology and Children* (University of London Press, 1973).

R. Mager, *Preparing Instructional Objectives* (Fearon Publishers, 1978).

Manpower Services Commission, *New Training Initiative: An Agenda for Action* (December, 1981).

M. Bigge, *Learning Theories for Teachers* (Harper and Row, 1975).

A. Rosson and S. Wanous, *Philosophy and Psychology of Teaching Typewriting* (South-western Publishing Co., 1973).

L. Skurnik and F. George, *Psychology for Everyman* (Penguin, 1969).

A. Welford, *Skilled Performance: Perceptual and Motor Skills* (Scott, Foresman & Co., 1976).

Yorkshire and Humberside Council for Further Education, *Handbook for Teachers* (n.d.).

Chapter 20 Preparing for the Faculty Diploma

HARRY BUTLER

The Faculty of Teachers in Commerce has a much longer track record than the RSA in the realm of teachers' shorthand examinations and they now have their own Teachers' Diploma in Teeline.

In some respects the Faculty requirements differ from those of the RSA in that training is not extended over two years. In theory at least, a prospective candidate need not decide to enter until just before the closing date, although such a move without careful training would be unwise.

Everything in this book, therefore, is of use to the prospective candidate for the Faculty Diploma, including Chapter 19 which has been written primarily with the RSA examination in view.

As with any other examination of credibility and standing, there are certain qualifications required by the Faculty before it can be taken. These are:

Educational requirements: GCE O level in English language; or the CSE equivalent; or the RSA Intermediate stage; or such equivalent qualification as the Diploma Examinations Board may approve.
Subject requirements: Possession of a speed certificate for at least 80 w.p.m. awarded by a recognized examining body.

The Faculty state that mature students over the age of 30 years who do not have these qualifications may apply to take the Diploma and each application is dealt with on its merits.

There is no necessity to undertake teaching under supervision for a given number of hours, as with the training course for the RSA, but it is suggested that a candidate should obtain as much teaching experience as possible and at least some of this should be under supervision. If a number of candidates are studying together for the Diploma, no doubt they will take turns at giving lessons, with the others taking the role of students and asking searching questions. In this way all will benefit, but of course there should also be an amount of actual class work with learners.

The Faculty examination is held twice a year, in May and November, and lasts approximately five hours. It is taken at centres arranged countrywide. There are four sections:

1. Specimen lesson

This is an oral test on one of two topics. A fortnight's notice is given of this and the candidate must prepare full lesson notes, a copy of which must be handed to the examiner. Half an hour is allowed for the oral part and although this may not be sufficient time in which to complete the lesson, it will be enough for the examiner to reach a decision. If the lesson does not go the full 30 minutes, it could well mean that the examiner is satisfied and requires no more; so if this happens the candidate should not be worried.

In preparing for this paper, candidates should remember that they will be required to give the lesson *as they would in a class.* Regard the examiner as a class that is being shown the principle for the first time. S/he will probably remain expressionless throughout, but do not be put off if this is so. The examiner is there to judge the candidate's ability, not to show whether a lesson is being put over rightly or wrongly.

It may be that the examiner will ask a candidate to imagine that half the lesson has already been given, and to continue from a later point. For example, if the subject is the CM blend, then the candidate may be told: 'You have already explained CAM and CEM; now continue to present your lesson from CIM onwards.' Or the candidate may get as far as CAM and begin to dictate some words covering that portion of the lesson when the examiner may quietly interrupt with 'Yes. Now let us assume that the dictation has been completed and continue with the next part of the lesson.'

Such interruptions should not be construed as an indication that the examiner is irritated or in any way bored by the method of presentation.

If the room is a large one, remember to pitch the voice so that a student in the back row would hear clearly, and write the outlines on the board so that they can be seen at the back. Address the imaginary class, and not the examiner.

Chalkboard technique is sometimes a weakness. Cultivate the habit, during training and mock lesson sessions, of standing to the side of the board so that students can see the outlines being written, and remember to talk to the class and not to the board.

At the end of the lesson, the chalkboard presentation should be as readable as the page of a book, beginning at the top left-hand corner and finishing at the bottom on the right – but do not go so far down the board that pupils at the back might be unable to see without craning their necks.

Some candidates may prefer to use an overhead projector rather than a chalkboard, but the foregoing comments still apply. The presentation must be neat and the progression logical.

A common failing is to 'rush' the lesson, as if to get it over and done with. Take your time. Other shortcomings are to talk too quickly and to drop the voice too much at the end of a sentence (remember those in the back row, and that aeroplane passing overhead!) Don't be afraid to use topical allusions or 'pop' song titles if they can be worked in, and if the lesson is being presented as to a class of teenagers.

The lesson plan which has to be given to the examiner should be detailed. It would be wise to indicate for whom the lesson is intended (whether sixth forms, evening classes, TOPS courses, etc.); to state the length of the course, objectives of the lesson and the length of the lesson; and remember, when preparing the plan, to allow time for students to practise. It should also state which textbook is being used. An example of a lesson plan can be seen on pages 116–17.

With all other papers in the examination, 10 minutes' reading time is allowed before work begins on that particular section.

2. Marking a student's exercise

The Faculty has made a change in this paper. Formerly it was a shorthand passage of continuous matter in which 12 or 15 words were either incorrectly written or were capable of being written a better way.

This paper will in future consist of two passages, printed as pages from a notebook, with a key alongside. The first passage will resemble the writing of a student who has just finished the theory. The second will simulate the note-taking of a student at 100–120 words a minute.

Candidates will be required to mark each passage and put the recommended outline in the margin for each outline they encircle in the notes. On a separate sheet of lined paper they will then comment on what they consider to be the five most important differences in each passage, giving guidance as they would to a student. This means they will comment on a total of 10 outlines instead of 8 as in previous examinations.

The time allowed for this paper is 1 hour (previously 45 minutes) plus 10 minutes' reading time.

Points to note are that if a word which is a standard special form has been written fully, it should be marked as incorrect; if an outline is capable of being written another and preferable way (i.e. if *warn* is written W-R-N instead of with the WRN blend) then it should be corrected, and the preferable way shown, together with two or three other examples.

The aim of this paper is to see if the candidate can quickly and efficiently mark an exercise, and give suitable guidance in the accompanying comments. It is not sufficient to comment on the one outline; other examples should be given as well. Thus, if the outline being commented upon is *warn*, then not only should the WRN blend be shown for the word, but similar examples should be included, such as *warns*, *warned*, *warning*, and there would be no harm if the candidate added 'see page . . . of your textbook'. The page number would have to be left blank, but no doubt the marker would appreciate your thoughtfulness and thoroughness in directing the student to the appropriate page of the textbook.

3. Longhand into shorthand

For this paper 20 minutes is allowed (plus 10 minutes' reading time). The candidate is presented with a continuous passage of about 240 words for putting into Teeline. Attention should be paid to a good, legible style of writing and to judicious grouping. The intention of the paper is to test the knowledge of rules and principles, and the knowledge of grouping.

Favourite 'short cuts', all very well in personal writing, should be avoided and only standard Teeline as shown in *Teeline Revised Edition* or *Teeline Shorthand Made Simple* should be used.

During training for this section, the candidate should do as much practice as possible. Avoid crossing out – and that means writing the proper outline the first time. One's shorthand improves with practice and there should be plenty of it for this paper. Nothing impresses a student more than a neat, tidy style, and the same might be said of the examiner.

4. The principles of teaching and their application to shorthand

This is a combined paper for which $2\frac{1}{2}$ hours are allowed, plus the 10 minutes' reading time. Of the questions on the paper, the candidate will be required to answer four: one on the general principles of teaching and three on the methods of teaching shorthand (see page 140 for guidance on further reading).

The heading for this paper is self-explanatory and the type of material covered is set out in the Faculty's handbook, *Regulations and Syllabuses for Teachers' Diplomas*, obtainable from the Examinations Secretary.

It should be emphasized again that where shorthand writing is required, only *standard* Teeline outlines should be used. With such a flexible system as Teeline it is perhaps inevitable that some teachers should have adopted their own pet outlines. Others have retained obsolete methods of writing that were used in the early days of Teeline but were subsequently found wanting for various reasons and were therefore discontinued. This comment applies especially to the letter B and to the use of an LF blend which at one time was a companion to the still-used FL blend. Without wishing to anticipate the views of the examiners, it is more than likely that any departure from standard Teeline as set out in the current textbooks would incur a penalty.